SEW SERENDIPITY

SEW SERENDIPITY

*Fresh + Pretty Designs
to Make and Wear*

KAY WHITT

KRAUSE PUBLICATIONS
CINCINNATI, OHIO

www.fwmedia.com

14   13   12   11   10   5   4   3   2   1

DISTRIBUTED IN CANADA BY FRASER DIRECT
100 Armstrong Avenue
Georgetown, ON, Canada L7G 5S4
Tel: (905) 877-4411

DISTRIBUTED IN THE U.K. AND EUROPE BY DAVID & CHARLES
Brunel House, Newton Abbot, Devon, TQ12 4PU, England
Tel: (+44) 1626 323200, Fax: (+44) 1626 323319
Email: postmaster@davidandcharles.co.uk

DISTRIBUTED IN AUSTRALIA BY CAPRICORN LINK
P.O. Box 704, S. Windsor NSW, 2756 Australia
Tel: (02) 4577-3555

Library of Congress Cataloging in Publication Data
Whitt, Kay.
  Sew serendipity : fresh + pretty designs to make and wear / Kay Whitt. -- 1st ed.
      p. cm.
  Includes bibliographical references and index.
  ISBN-13: 978-1-4402-0357-2 (hardcover : alk. paper)
  ISBN-10: 1-4402-0357-1 (hardcover : alk. paper)
  1. Dressmaking. I. Title.
  TT515.W426 2010
  646.4'04--dc22
                                        2010008060

Edited by Vanessa Lyman
Designed by Michelle Thompson
Production coordinated by Greg Nock
Step-by-step photography by Christine Polomsky, all other
      photography by Ric Deliantoni
Illustrations and samples created by Kay Whitt

Metric Conversion Chart

To convert	to	multiply by
Inches	Centimeters	2.54
Centimeters	Inches	0.4
Feet	Centimeters	30.5
Centimeters	Feet	0.03
Yards	Meters	0.9
Meters	Yards	1.1

About the Author

"Love what you do, and you will never work a day in your life."

In a nutshell, this quote describes exactly the way Kay Whitt feels about her work as a pattern designer for clothing and accessories. After spending nine years as an elementary school teacher (sewing in her spare time and selling her creations to colleagues), she resigned from teaching and launched her pattern company. Since then, Kay has earned a reputation for her innovative designs and clear instructions, making her patterns some of the most popular in the marketplace.

In addition to the designs she creates for her company, Serendipity Studio (www.sewserendipity.com), she is a licensed designer for the McCall Pattern Company as Kay Whitt Designs.

Kay resides in Texas with her husband, Keith, and their two birds, ET and Zeppy. She is always busy working on something new and exciting and never tires of sharing her passion for design and sewing.

Dedication

This book is dedicated to my mother, who instilled the love of sewing in me from the time I was a little girl.

Acknowledgments

A very special thanks to the following wonderful people—To my husband, Keith: Thank you for your tireless support and encouragement, even when the house was a mess of thread, fabric snippets, and other assorted little nightmares—you're the best! To my Monday Girls, Clarees, Leslie, and Marsha: Thanks for your wonderful friendship and enthusiasm. Your support has meant so much to me on this journey! To my editor, Vanessa: Thanks for sharing my vision and always working on my behalf to get this book to absolute perfection. Your guidance has been invaluable! To Outlaw at Moda/United Notions: Thanks so much for letting me come out to visit and bum fabulous fabrics from you. Your generosity has been phenomenal! To Kathy at Michael Miller Fabrics: I love your enthusiasm and appreciate your unbelievable generosity in providing me with my heart's content of your much beloved fabrics. To Miranda Weeks McGahey: thanks for the contribution of your lovely hand-dyed wool and linens for two of the jackets—it makes them extra special. To Nancy at Checker: thank you for your support of my designs and the belief that this book was a great idea! To my friends at Bernina USA: Thanks a million for loaning the machines for the photography portion of the book. I loved getting to use ones just like I have at home. I know there are probably many others that I have not mentioned here, but know that this book would not have been possible without all of you, and for that, I sincerely thank you from the bottom of my heart.

Contents

Introduction

WELCOME TO *Sew Serendipity*!

Making clothing has the reputation of being intimidating. I have heard time and time again many of you are great at making bags and other accessories, but when it comes to clothing, you simply fall apart! This does not have to be the case. In many ways, clothing is *so* forgiving. The seams need to be fairly consistent, but if you make one seam just slightly bigger or smaller than another, no one is going to know. It isn't the same sort of precision that is required to make a quilt. (I'm horrible about that—my quarter-inch seams are never all alike!)

I love making clothing, partially because garments are just so fast to make! Once you have mastered a set of instructions for any given project, you can lay it out, cut it up, sew it up, and put it on!

Notice how many of the projects have been paired together. I want you to feel that these clothes can be a valuable extension of your current wardrobe. Mix and match tunics and dresses with jackets and jackets with skirts to create your own signature look.

I love to come up with a basic design and see how many different ways I can express it, which is why I offer so many variations in my company's pattern line. I took this idea and applied it to the clothing projects you will find here.

Here's how it works. The next few pages address measuring, tools of the trade, and some specific garment sewing skills.

Then, you'll move into the projects section. At the beginning of each clothing section, you will find a set of General Construction steps. These are the "master steps" that cover how the garment will be sewn together. Then with each individual project you will find the detailed steps that make that one unique. These two groups of instructions will be used together to make whichever variation you choose, so there will be some flipping back and forth between the two. The best part about making the instructions in this way is that when you have mastered the construction for one version, then all the variations are a snap because they all are put together the same way.

The projects in the book are also arranged according to skill level. If you are a beginning sewer, start with a skirt design, then progress on to tunics and dresses, then jackets.

I've included details on how to lay the tissue pieces onto the fabric, as well as advice on making each project uniquely your own. I want you to feel that you can be creative with these designs and make them to fit your individual style. In other words, be your own designer and have fun!

Steps to a Custom Fit

Let's face it, not all bodies are created equal. Even if you wear a size medium and your best friend does too, your bodies are simply not the same.

Most pattern companies establish a "norm" on which they base their patterns. This means that they pick a standardized length for arms, legs, waist size, back length, hips and shoulder slope, etc., for each size. When working with a commercial pattern, this can be where the frustration sets in. Very few commercial patterns will be just right because of the unique qualities of each human body. This is why measuring your body and making a "muslin" of the garment you want to make is so important.

If you aren't familiar with the term "muslin," it simply means that you make a sample of the garment from muslin fabric. (Muslin is plain, inexpensive fabric that has no pattern so you can focus on the fitting. However, if you have a piece of fabric that doesn't thrill you, use it for the sample garment in order to put it to good use.) With a muslin, you can adjust the fit before starting on the "real" project. It will take some extra time, but it is *so* worth it in the long run.

But the first step in achieving a custom fit is taking your measurements. Having a friend help out during the measuring process makes it easier. Have a measuring party! Be sure to record each measurement as you take it. See the drawing on the next page for the measurements you need.

Once your measurements are taken, you can make your muslin. Refer to the chart on page 13 to determine which size pattern from the enclosed pattern sheets will work best. If you are between sizes on the chart, err on larger side—it's easier to trim. Cut out the pattern pieces, pin them to the muslin, and cut out the pieces. Assemble the muslin following the General Construction steps for your particular project. If something doesn't work, adjust the muslin, and mark the change on the pattern pieces.

make it your own

A custom fit is just the first step to customizing. Customizing the style is another way to make each design uniquely yours. Throughout the book, you'll find "Make It Your Own" sidebars, that give you tips on choosing fabrics or adding embellishments to change it up! Don't hesitate to take inspiration from one project and use it on another—what about a little tie bow at the hem of a tunic? Or adding rosettes to a neckline? Learn to customize beyond the size!

CUSTOM FITTING
Taking Measurements

To work with the patterns in this book, you need your bust, waist and hip measurements. The other measurements are useful for adjusting the patterns. To get started measuring your body, you need a good dressmaker's measuring tape. When you measure, you need to be as close to your skin as possible to make measurements. Measurements made over clothing will not be accurate. Be sure that you are wearing a good supportive bra, not necessarily a push-up bra, unless you wear one on a consistent basis.

Bust: To measure around the bust, wrap the measuring tape around the fullest part of your bustline, making sure that the tape is not sagging in the back. Pull the tape taut, but not overly tight.

Waist: Tie a thin strip of fabric at your natural waistline to locate it, then use the measuring tape to take the measurement. Drop down about 2" from the natural waist and measure again. This is the below-waist measurement, or high hip; a lot of women find this the most comfortable place for skirts to sit. It also compliments the majority of figures because it gives the appearance of a longer torso.

Hips: Measure around the fullest part of the hips. Be sure that the measuring tape is not riding too high or low along your back side.

Arm Length: Measure the length of your arm starting at the top of your shoulder and down past your wrist to the base of the thumb. The reason you don't stop at the wrist is that the full-length sleeve will appear too short when your arm is bent. Also measure for a three-quarter-length sleeve and for a bracelet-length sleeve, which is at or slightly above the wrist.

Skirt Length: Measure from your preferred waistline down to above the knee, below the knee, and mid-calf. There will probably be one or two lengths that suit your body type the best; use your personal judgement when cutting the lengths for the skirt projects. Note that the skirt projects in this book are based on an A-line, which compliments the majority of body types.

Jacket Length: Start measuring at the base of your neck at the center back and record the measurements at the high hip. Be sure to stop just before the fullest part of the hip; a jacket that hits the body at the fullest point is not the most complimentary to many figures. Continue measuring to the fingertip length, then on to the below-knee length. The jacket projects in this book have a wide variety of lengths. You'll find these measurements valuable when deciding on a cutting length.

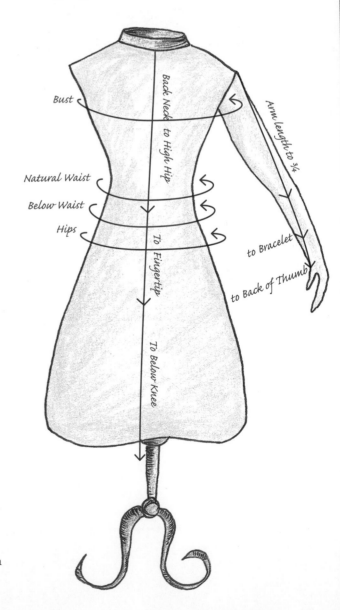

Making the Muslin

At this point, you have the measurements that will be needed for determining the best size to start the muslin. Begin the custom fitting process by looking at the size chart on this page. If you find that your measurements fall between two sizes, use the larger of the two. You may have to take it in here and there, but if you start too small, there is no place to go.

If you're making the skirt, choose the size listed that fits your hips the best—the waist can be adjusted to accommodate your individual needs. If you're making the jacket or tunic/dress, select the size by using the bust measurement that works the best for you.

Once you have determined your size, take a look at the enclosed tissue pattern sheets. Each piece includes a ½" seam allowance unless otherwise noted. (Some of the facings may not be labeled with sizes due to space restrictions; keep in mind that the innermost line is XXS and the outermost line is XXL.)

Begin by making a muslin. Treat it just like you would the actual project. Cut out the tissue pattern pieces for your size. (When you cut out your pieces, I recommend leaving all the size lines intact. In the event you want to adjust the size, you'll have what you need.) Pin the pieces onto the muslin, and then cut out the fabric pieces. Set the tissue pieces aside. You'll be marking any adjustments made to the muslin onto these pieces. Assemble the fabric pieces following the General Construction instructions for the project.

When you make your muslin, you don't have to worry about all of the topstitching and finishing touches. The focus is on getting the best possible fit. A lot of people like to sew muslins with the seams facing outward so that alterations can be measured and recorded. If you find the seams distracting, make the garment with the seams to the inside and take note of the alterations as you go. It is *very* important to keep detailed notes of the changes you make so that these changes can be applied when you make the garment from the fabric you love. It will make the sewing process easier, faster and fun.

I suggest that you use a straight stitch with a long stitch length and keep all of the seam allowances intact (no trimming). Try the garment on often to check the progress of the fit. As you adjust the fit of the muslin, mark the changes on the tissue pattern pieces. It is *not* necessary to add facings to the muslin for the jacket and skirt, but keep in mind that if you change anything about the front (such as for the jacket), the facings will need to have the same changes so that they'll fit properly. When creating a muslin for the tunic/dress, you *will* need to add the facings, since elastic needs to be inserted for the proper sleeve fit.

Make one more muslin reflecting all of the adjustments before making the first garment. If major changes have been made, use pattern tracing cloth or non-fusible interfacing to trace and cut new pieces that reflect these changes. Be sure to label each piece with the necessary darts and notches as well as the pattern piece name so that they can be re-used easily in the future.

Size Chart

To determine which size pattern to use from the enclosed pattern sheets, refer to these measurements.

	XXS	XS	S	M	L	XL	XXL
Bust	32"	34"	36"	38"	40"	42"	44"
Waist	24"	26"	28"	30"	32"	34"	36"
Hip	34"	36"	38"	40"	42"	44"	46"

Adjusting the Fit

These are some of the more common adjustments you might find yourself making to the pattern pieces when adjusting them. Once you make a muslin and adjust the fit, transfer the corrections to the pattern pieces.

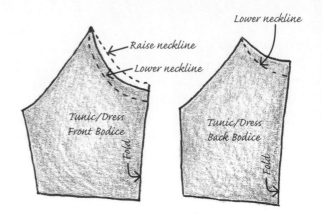

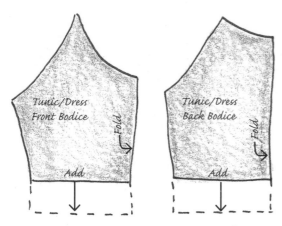

Bodice of tunic pieces are shown. This technique can also be applied to the Jacket Bodice.

Bodice Length: If you are large busted, you may need more length on the bodice to accommodate your shape. This is completed by extending the lower line of the bodice as shown. The gathering at the bodice should provide some extra width. However, if you find lengthening the bodice was not enough, you can add width to the Front Bodice. If you do, make sure to add width to the Front Facing as well.

Neckline and Shoulders: Watch how the shoulders fit. Since the jacket projects are based on a raglan sleeve, they are super forgiving, and look great on just about anyone. Check the neckline on the tunic/dress and make adjustments if you feel that the neckline rides too low in the front or too high in the back. Note the changes that could be made to these pieces (indicated on the illustration above).

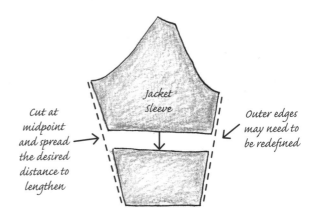

Sleeve Length: Take a look at the sleeve length. If you would like them longer or shorter, take note of how this alteration could look for either the jacket or tunic/dress. Note on the jacket that if you want to lengthen the sleeve you will need to cut the sleeve apart and add the length at close to the midpoint rather than at the hemline due to the tapered nature of the sleeve. If you have particularly long arms, double-check the length before cutting the pieces from fabric.

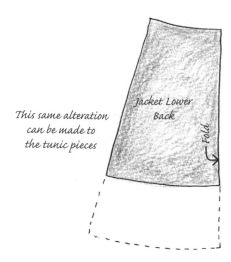

This same alteration can be made to the tunic pieces

Jacket Lower Back

Fold

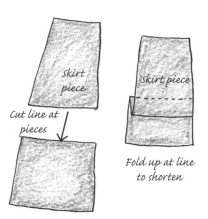

skirt piece

Cut line at pieces

skirt piece

Fold up at line to shorten

This represents the process for all of the skirt pieces

Tunic/Dress or Jacket Length: If you want to shorten or lengthen the tunic/dress or jacket, add to or subtract from the bottom cutting line. This may simply mean that you are choosing a spot lower than what is printed on the tissue. If you'd like to add even more length to the longest tunic/dress or jacket, you can certainly do that, but take into account that the sides are angled and will need to be adjusted as shown. If you are long-legged or have a longer torso, you may need additional fabric to achieve the desired length.

Skirt Length: There are horizontal lines drawn on each skirt piece for shortening or lengthening. Fold up on this line to shorten the skirt or cut the pieces apart on this line and add inches to extend the length as shown.

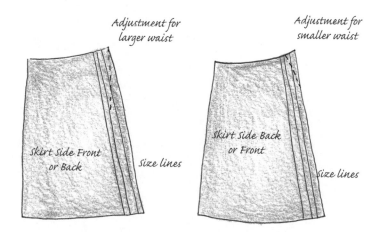

Adjustment for larger waist

Adjustment for smaller waist

Skirt Side Front or Back

size lines

Skirt Side Back or Front

size lines

Make adjustments to both Side Front and Side Back pieces

Hip/Waist Adjustment: Based on your personal measurements, there may be a discrepancy between the hips and waist with regard to the size chart. As instructed earlier, use the size that best fits your hips, then adjust the waist accordingly to fit as shown.

Sewing Machine and Accessories

Perhaps the most important tool of all is your sewing machine. A machine can really make or break your sewing experience, which is why it is so important to get the best one you can afford. Even if you have to forego the bells and whistles, get a basic machine from a reputable company. You will have considerably less trouble and enjoy your sewing, which is what it's all about, after all!

I sew with Bernina machines, which I dearly love. I have an Aurora 430 that does just about all of the major work and I also have a Bernina 1150MDA serger.

It's important at some point to purchase a serger if you plan on doing much garment sewing. It will really raise the quality of your sewing to a professional level. I have owned a serger for nearly ten years and kicked myself for not owning one sooner—they are *so* worth the investment!

- - - -- - -- - MACHINE FEET - - -- - -- - -

Open-Toe Embroidery Foot: Believe it or not, this is the foot (1) that I do *all* of my sewing with. The reason for that is because I love to be able to fully see where the needle is at all times. This ingenious foot allows me that luxury, so my regular sewing foot never really gets any use.

Denim Foot: This foot (2) is ideal for sewing through many layers of fabric and stabilizer. It gives additional support to the needle and thus you have less needle breakage.

Teflon-Coated Foot: This foot (3) is great for sewing with vinyl-coated cottons. It enables the fabric to flow easily under the machine foot instead of getting caught up as with a regular foot. If you plan on doing much sewing with this type of fabric or with other synthetic fabrics, this is the best foot for the job.

Zipper Foot: This foot (4) is indispensable for adding zippers to garments or bags. It's possible to use the regular zipper foot for sewing invisible zippers, so be sure you have checked that out in the Sewing Techniques section.

Ruffler Attachment: I love this machine attachment (5)! It's a bit expensive, but it saves time and gives you perfect ruffles every time without having to pull up those pesky bobbin threads.

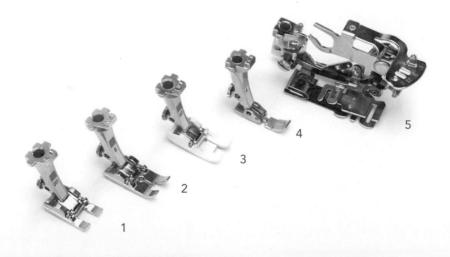

Indispensable Notions

Aside from a machine in good working order, here are some tools and notions that I consider indispensable.

STABILIZERS

Interfacing: I can't say enough about interfacing. When I began sewing, I hated it! I always whined about the extra step and my mother would always say, "Well, you could leave it out, but it won't look the same..." I knew what that meant, so I always bucked up and added it. What a difference it makes!

I personally prefer the Pellon products, but use what you like best.

Fusible Interfacing: Pellon fusible interfacing is 20" wide and sold by the yard. I use the one specifically made for light- to medium-weight fabrics. It's fusible on one side. Quite often I use a single layer of this stabilizer for linings and pockets. Even though I use heavier fabrics for some of the jackets, I still prefer to use this lighter interfacing. It reinforces and defines without adding bulk.

MEASURING TOOLS

Dressmaker's Measuring Tape: This tape (1) is about 60" long and is very flexible. It's perfect for taking body measurements and other varied measuring uses when you need a flexible tool.

Dressmaker's Adjustable Ruler: This is a 6"-long ruler (2) usually made of metal with a small slider. This is great to use when marking a hem or trimming fabric from the bottom of a jacket, skirt or sleeve.

Quilting Ruler: I love my 24" × 6" quilting ruler (3)! It is transparent so I can use it for a variety of measuring needs. I use it often for cutting strips of fabric with my mat and rotary cutter. Even if you don't quilt, this is a great tool.

MARKING TOOLS

Marking Pencils: There are a variety of tools out there, from chalk pencils to air-soluble markers. I've recently discovered Sewline marking pencils (4). What can I say about these pencils? They're the best! They work like a mechanical pencil with a retractable lead and even come with a handy eraser that really does remove the marks from the fabric. They come in a variety of colors. I have tried many marking pencils over the years, and these are, hands-down, the best. These can be purchased at your local quilt shop or online.

IRONS & IRONING BOARDS

Irons: I have a Rowenta Steam Generator. If you do a lot of ironing, you need this tool. It has fantastic steam power which makes ironing so easy! It holds four cups of water in the tank, which is about 1½ solid hours of steam. This means you can pretty much sew all day and not run out of steam. How is that for awesome?

Ironing Board: I have a Rowenta Professional Ironing Board—I love this little beauty! It features an extra-wide board, making it a great location to lay out pieces to get them ready for ironing. It also has a shelf to the side for holding the iron and a lower shelf for holding other items. It's heavy duty and well balanced so that it does not tip easily.

Sleeve Board: A sleeve board (5) looks like a mini-ironing board. It's just wonderful for pressing sleeve facings and bands in place without creasing the sleeve anywhere.

Pressing Cloth: I use a plain white tea towel as a pressing cloth. A pressing cloth is invaluable when working with heat-sensitive materials, such as laminated or napped fabrics (like velvet or velveteen).

Scissors: I have three pairs of 6" Gingher scissors (6). I keep them stashed at different locations in my studio so that a pair is always handy. These are tough scissors that retain their sharpness for a long time and can cut through many layers of fabric at once. They have great points which help to clip curves and snip into seam allowances where needed.

Thread Snips: I love having a pair of thread snips (7) by the machine to clip threads. They fit easily into your hand and are ergonomically friendly.

Rotary Cutter and Mat: I use my rotary cutter (8) and mat all the time. These tools, along with a quilting ruler, really are the best way to cut accurate squares, rectangles and strips.

Seam Ripper: It is inevitable that you will need a seam ripper (9) from time to time to do some "un-sewing." Not fun, but sometimes necessary. I also like to use these for opening buttonholes; be careful if you do—these are very sharp and can cut beyond the end of the buttonhole!

Point Turner: I use a bamboo skewer (10) or an acrylic point turner (11) to fully turn out pieces. Because both of these have a duller point than scissors, you're less likely to punch through a corner. I keep two or three acrylic point turners on hand in the studio at all times.

Pins: I use a variety of different-sized safety pins to turn tubes of fabric right side out. A lot of people like to use different turning tools, but I prefer the good old safety pin for this task. And I always have a supply of dressmaker's pins on hand (12). I like the ones with the pearlized heads—they are extra-long and very sharp

Pattern Tracing Cloth: This is a nylon product (13) that is translucent with a grid of dots spaced 1" apart. It's virtually impossible to tear, making it superior to using tissue scraps for tracing newly altered pattern pieces. You can write on it with pencil or pen and it can be gently pressed with low heat. It comes pre-packaged in 5-yard lengths or can be purchased by the yard and it is 36" wide.

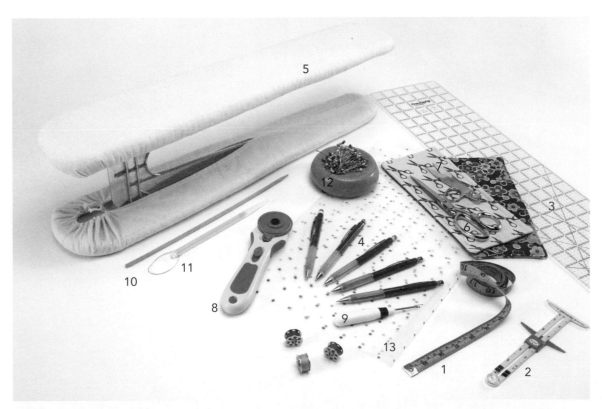

Pressing Intentional Creases

Many of the projects in the book are pressed specifically to create creases in the fabric. By doing this, ruffles lie flat and jackets made from heavier fabrics lie close to the body for a complimentary appearance.

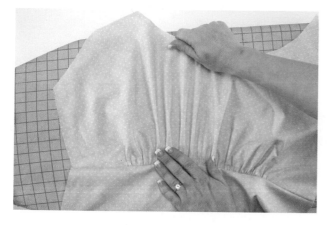

1. Lay out the piece that you want to press creases into on top of your ironing board. Fold the fabric by hand to gather it up as desired.

2. Apply a hot steam iron to the surface of the fabric, pressing in the creases. Use a pressing cloth for delicate fabrics as necessary.

Double Topstitching

Double topstitching both secures a seam and serves as a decorative detail. Choose a contrasting thread to make the topstitching stand out, or a matching thread to add a subtle bit of visual interest.

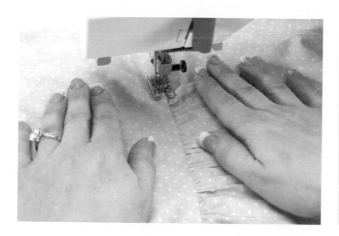

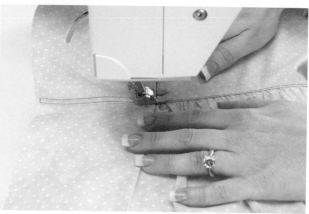

1. Begin by stitching along a finished edge or seam. (Note: I use an open-toe embroidery foot so that I can see the needle position at all times.)

2. Stitch again ¼" away from the first row of stitching. Use the outer edge of the foot as a guide to keep your stitching straight.

Installing an Invisible Zipper

Knowing how to insert an invisible zipper is a skill you'll always be grateful to have.

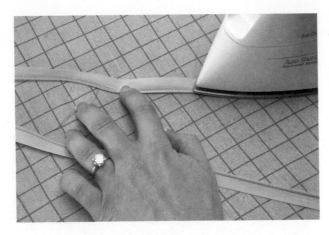

1. To prepare the garment opening for the zipper, serge or zigzag the raw edges of each garment piece. Mark the zipper placement at either ⅝" below the top edge or 3" below the top edge for the tunic/dress. Do not sew the seam. Open the zipper and turn it, right side against the ironing board. Press the zipper teeth away from the zipper tape.

2. Place the right side of the zipper, face down, against the right side of the fabric. Pin in place. Position the needle to the far right so that the needle is not hitting the foot and is close to the zipper teeth. Sew down one side of the zipper, to the zipper slide.

3. For the tunic/dress, close the zipper and mark the bust seam on the wrong side of the zipper tape. Unzip the zipper.

4. Place the right side of the remaining zipper tape against the other right side of the garment. If sewing the tunic/dress, match the mark on the zipper tape to the seam and pin.

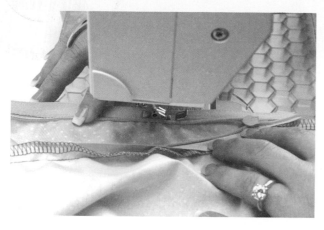

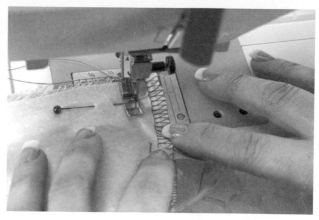

5. Be sure that the top of the zipper is even with the other side. Adjust the needle position to the far left so that the needle clears the foot and is close to the zipper teeth. Stitch in place.

6. Close the zipper to make sure the seams are lining up properly. Adjust the needle position to the far right and stitch the bottom portion of the seam, starting at the lower edge, with the raw edges against the ⅝" marking on the needle plate of the machine.

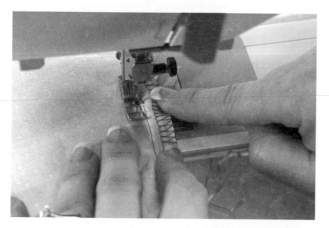

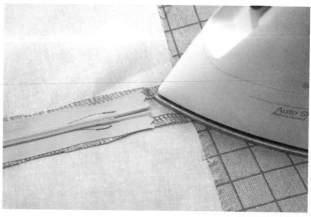

7. Keep stitching until you stitch onto the lower edge of the zipper tape. Repeat for the upper edge if you're making a tunic/dress.

8. Open the lower seam and carefully press the seams open.

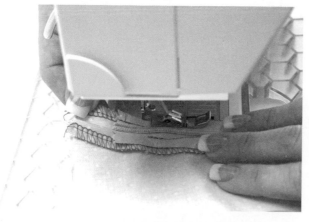

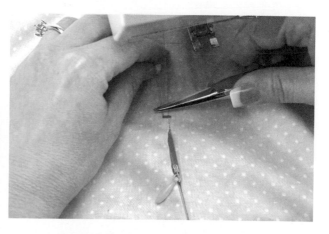

9. Stitch the lower portion of the zipper tape to just the seam allowance; this prevents the bottom of the zipper from flapping. Press the fabric to either side of the zipper to ensure everything lies flat.

10. For the tunic/dress, bartack at the top of the zipper to reinforce the seam using a very tight zigzag stitch. Clip away any loose threads.

Adding Facings

Facings help create a finished garment that hangs the way it should. All of the projects in this book use facings, so it's important to know how to add them, as well as how and when to clip a curve and trim a seam.

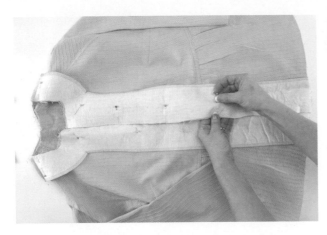

1. To add facings, place them along the outside of the garment, right sides together. Match sleeve seams for tunic/dress, side seams for skirt, or front edges for jacket. Pin in place, easing in any extra fullness as necessary.

2. Sew the facing to the garment with a ½" seam allowance. In the case of the jacket, continue stitching down the center fronts.

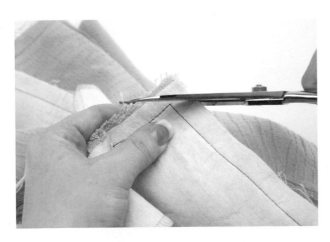

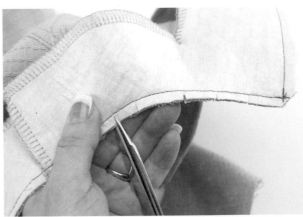

3. For the jacket, cut the top center front corners diagonally within the seam allowance.

4. To make seams lie flat and look professional, trim them down to ¼". In the case of inward curves, clip the seam allowance so the curve lies smoothly when turned right side out. In the case of scallops and other outward curves, it's helpful to cut wedges or notch the seam allowance so the bulk is removed and it lies flat when turned.

Understitching

Understitching is the process of securing the facings to the garment so that they will not roll out to the front side during wear.

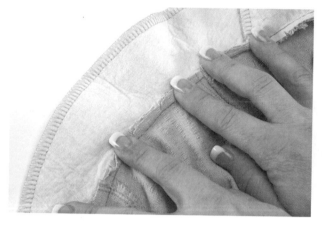

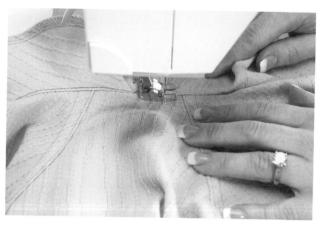

1. To understitch, open out the facing away from the garment, with the seam allowance turned toward the facing.

2. With the facing right side up, stitch close to the seam on the facing side, catching the seam allowance in the stitching. For the jacket, stitch as close to the center front corners as possible on the facing side.

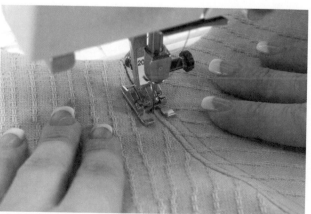

3. Turn the facings to the inside of the garment and press. For the skirt, turn in the seam allowance to either side of the zipper.

4. Edge- and topstitch as the project instructions indicate, then anchor the facing on the jacket by stitching-in-the-ditch along the sleeve seams. For the skirt, stitch-in-the-ditch on the side seams to anchor to facings.

Making Gathers

Ruffles and gathers are a great way to add fullness to a pattern, adding a sweet flirty twist. Gathers are used frequently throughout this book, especially at the bodice and sleeves.

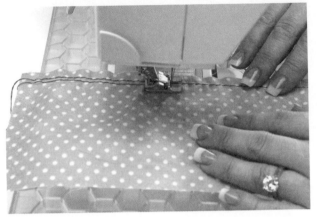

1. Using a long straight stitch, sew about ¼" away from the raw edge.

2. Sew another line of long, straight stitches about ⅜" away from the edge.

3. Wind the bobbin threads around your fingers and gently pull the threads to create gathers in the fabric. Keep pulling and positioning the gathers along the length of the fabric until you achieve the fullness you want.

Using a Ruffler Attachment

The ruffler attachment allows you to make uniform gathers or pleats with the sewing machine rather than pulling threads by hand.

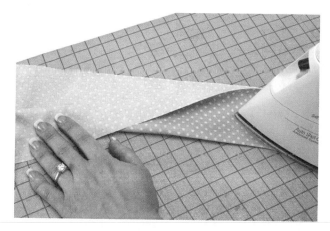

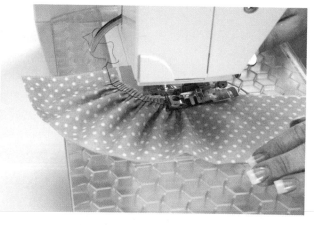

1. Most of the ruffles for the projects are created from a strip that has been folded in half lengthwise, wrong sides together, and pressed.

2. Place the strip between the blades on the ruffler attachment and using a straight stitch, sew about ¼"–⅜" from the raw edges. The individual project will detail whether to set the attachment to gather at every stitch or every 6th stitch.

3. Adjust the ruffles by hand, if needed, smoothing them out to make them easy to work with.

4. Press the ruffles flat to create a more pleated appearance.

Chapter One
SKIRTS

I LOVE A GREAT SKIRT! It's the perfect way to stay cool on hot summer days, yet look sophisticated. I especially love the way a skirt can bring together a collection of fabric prints in just the right way. With the skirts featured here, you can achieve a casual look while out and about running errands, or look quite elegant for a special evening by pairing it with one of the jackets.

The skirts in this section are all based on one set of pattern pieces for an A-line six-panel skirt. Once you have made yourself familiar with the General Construction techniques, you can make any of these skirts easily. Through the use of various fabric combinations and embellishments, each showcases a unique style and yet remains simple to sew. Once you have mocked up this design following the recommendations in Custom Fitting, you'll have a pattern design that is perfect for you.

Be creative with your fabric choices. For this design, I suggest 100% cotton quilting fabrics, linen or silk. I love pairing a great texture with cotton—silk with cotton is one of my personal favorites!

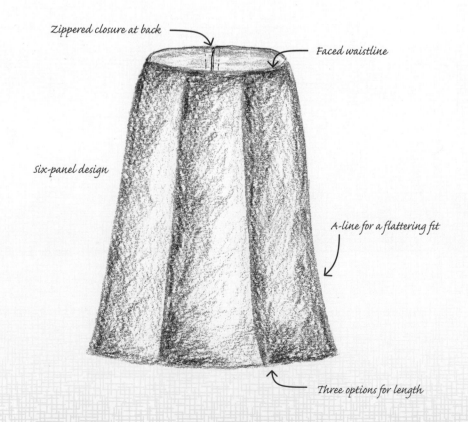

Zippered closure at back

Faced waistline

Six-panel design

A-line for a flattering fit

Three options for length

GENERAL CONSTRUCTION

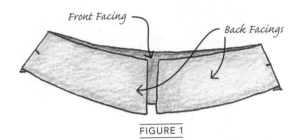

Front Facing

Back Facings

FIGURE 1

Right side of facing unit

Lower finished edge

FIGURE 2

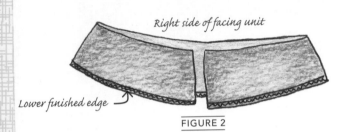

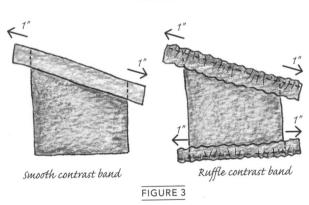

1"

1"

1"

1"

1"

1"

Smooth contrast band

Ruffle contrast band

FIGURE 3

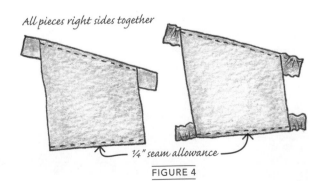

All pieces right sides together

¼" seam allowance

FIGURE 4

Once all the fabric pattern pieces have been cut and all notches have been marked or clipped, remove the tissue pattern pieces.

NOTE: All seam allowances are ½" unless otherwise stated.

- - - PREPARE THE WAISTLINE FACING - - -

1. Apply fusible interfacing to the wrong sides of Front and Back Facings following the manufacturer's instructions.

2. Matching notches, pin the Back Facings to the Front Facing, right sides together. (figure 1)

3. Sew ½" seams and press open. Finish the lower edge of the facing unit by serging or using a zigzag stitch. Set the facing unit aside. (figure 2)

- - - - - - MAKE THE POCKET - - - - - -

1. If making one pocket, cut out two Pocket pieces. If making two pockets, cut out four Pocket pieces.

2. Apply either the smooth or ruffle contrast fabric band (as directed in the variation you are making) to the top edge of the Pocket piece, right sides together, matching the raw edges. The contrast band should extend 1" beyond each side edge. (figure 3)

3. Sew the contrast fabric band to the Pocket piece with a ¼" seam allowance.

4. With right sides together, lay the remaining Pocket piece on top. Follow the previous stitching along the top edge and stitch a ¼" seam along the bottom. Leave side edges open. (figure 4)

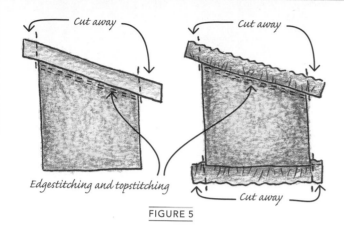

Cut away

Cut away

Edgestitching and topstitching

Cut away

FIGURE 5

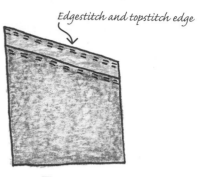

Edgestitch and topstitch edge

FIGURE 6

5. Turn the pocket right side out and press the seams at the top and bottom. Press the contrast fabric band or ruffle away from the pocket to extend beyond the pocket edge. Edgestitch and topstitch the upper pocket edge on the main fabric below the seam. (figure 5)

6. For the smooth contrast fabric band, edge- and topstitch the band along the pressed edges. (figure 6)

7. Pin the pocket to the Side Front piece, right side up. For one pocket, pin to the left Side Front. For two pockets, place one on each Side Front. All pieces should have right sides facing up. Place the pocket on the skirt so that the upper slanting seam is about 3½" down from the top edge of the skirt and the lower slanting seam is about 6" down from the top edge of the skirt. (figure 7)

8. Sew the side edges of the pocket in place, using a ¼" seam. Edgestitch along the bottom on the main fabric. Topstitch along the bottom edge of the pocket as well. Trim the contrast fabric band or ruffle edges that extend beyond the Side Front edge. (figure 8)

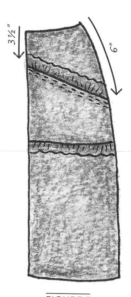

3½"

6"

FIGURE 7

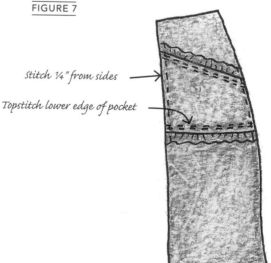

Stitch ¼" from sides

Topstitch lower edge of pocket

FIGURE 8

31

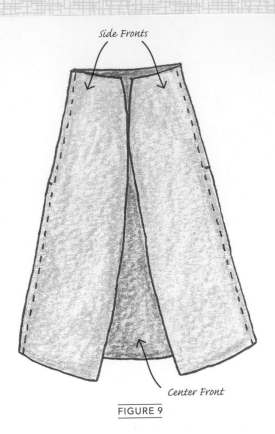

Side Fronts

Center Front

FIGURE 9

SEW THE SKIRT SECTIONS AND ADD THE ZIPPER

1. With right sides together, matching notches and top and bottom edges, place a Side Front on each side of the Center Front. Pin, then stitch together. (figure 9) These seams can be serged together or trimmed and zigzagged to keep the edges from ravelling.

2. Press the seams toward the Center Front and edge-stitch close to the seam on the Center Front piece.

3. Place one Side Back on each of the Center Back skirt pieces, right sides together. Match the notches as well as the top and bottom edges. Sew and press the seam toward the Center Back piece. Edgestitch the seams. Keep the Center Back open to prepare for the zipper installation. (figure 10)

4. Edge finish each Center Back edge and install the zipper (page 22) according to the instructions in the Sewing Techniques section. (figure 11)

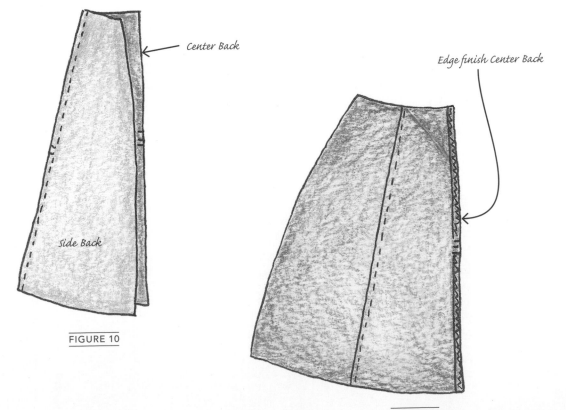

Center Back

Side Back

FIGURE 10

Edge finish Center Back

FIGURE 11

SEW THE SIDE SEAMS
AND ADD THE FACINGS

1. Once the zipper has been installed and the seam is sewn and pressed, place the front and back skirt sections right sides together. Make sure the side seams are aligned, the notches are matched, and the edges at the top and bottom are even. Sew each side seam and press the seam to one side. (figure 12) Clip the curve of the seam near the top as necessary.

2. Edgestitch the side seams, as before, close to the seamline.

3. Unzip the skirt and open out the top edge at the zipper. Add the facings to the top edge of the skirt, right sides together with back edges even, matching side seams. (figure 13)

4. Sew the facing to the skirt. Trim the seam to ¼" and clip the seam allowance. (figure 14)

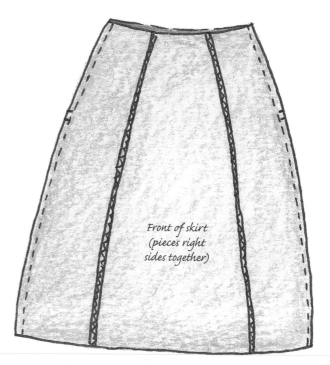

Front of skirt (pieces right sides together)

FIGURE 12

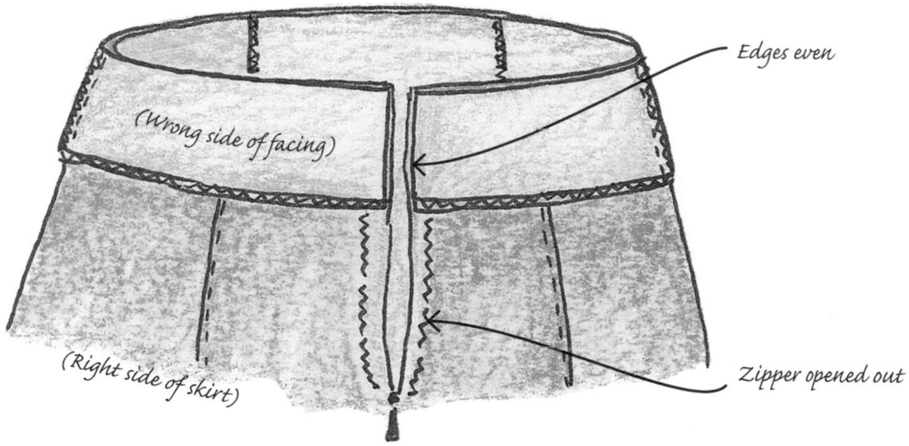

Edges even

(Wrong side of facing)

(Right side of skirt)

Zipper opened out

FIGURE 13

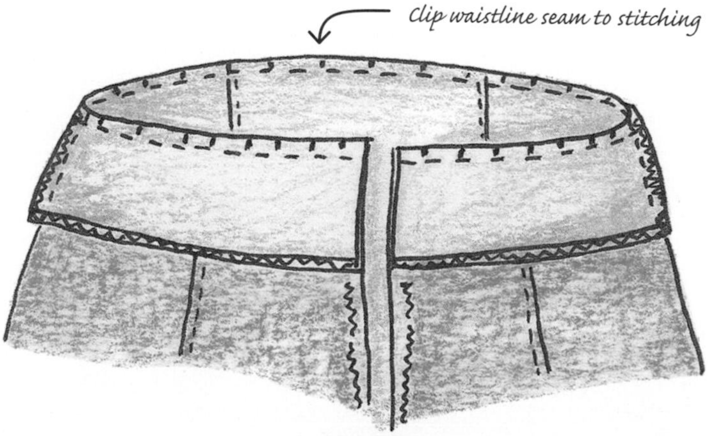

Clip waistline seam to stitching

FIGURE 14

33

5. Understitch the facing as instructed in the Sewing Techniques section (page 25).

6. Turn the facing to the inside of the skirt and press. Close the zipper and open out the facings at Center Back. Fold in the ends of the facing ½" and gently press. Turn the facing back to the inside and press again. (figures 15a, 15b)

7. Edgestitch the top finished edge of the skirt through all thicknesses. (figure 16)

- - - - - ADD THE LOWER SKIRT - - - - -

1. Sew the skirt's Lower Back Panel piece to the Lower Front Panel piece along the side seams. Keep right sides together, and match notches and edges. (figure 17) Press seams to one side.

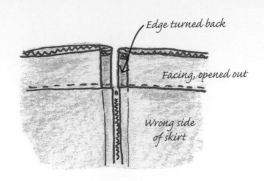

Edge turned back

Facing, opened out

Wrong side of skirt

FIGURE 15A

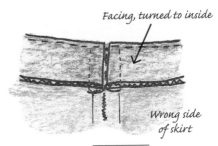

Facing, turned to inside

Wrong side of skirt

FIGURE 15B

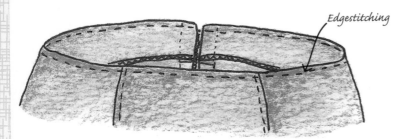

Edgestitching

FIGURE 16

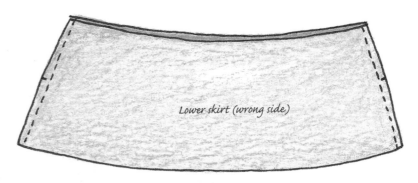

Lower skirt (wrong side)

FIGURE 17

2. Pin and stitch the lower skirt to the main skirt, right sides together, matching notches and side seams. (figure 18)

3. Press the seam toward the main skirt. Edgestitch next to the seam on top of the seam allowance and also topstitch if desired.

- -- --- --- **HEM THE SKIRT** - --- --- -

1. Clean finish the lower edge of the skirt with the serger, or use a zigzag stitch. Turn up a 1" hem, wrong sides together, and press. (figure 19)

2. From the right side of the fabric, topstitch along the bottom edge of the skirt, once ¾" away from the pressed edge, and then again ⅝" from the edge. Press the hem. (figure 20)

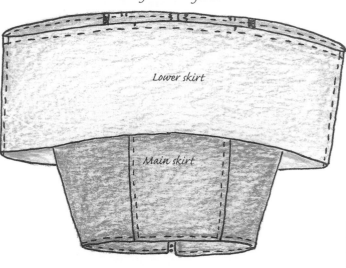

Pieces right sides together

Lower skirt

Main skirt

FIGURE 18

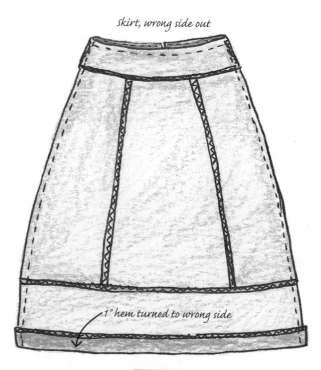

Skirt, wrong side out

1" hem turned to wrong side

FIGURE 19

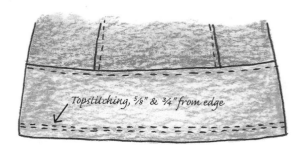

Topstitching, ⅝" & ¾" from edge

FIGURE 20

APPLIQUÉ SKIRT

Materials list

Main Fabric

All sizes: 1⅛ yards
(45"-wide fabric) or 1 yard
(60"-wide fabric)

Contrast Fabric

All sizes: ⅝ yard (45"-wide
fabric) or ⅓ yard (60"-wide
fabric)

Other Supplies

¼ yard of 20"-wide fusible
interfacing for light- to
medium-weight fabrics

9" invisible zipper

Polyester machine thread to
match fabrics

Small sequins
(approximately 100)

Rotary cutter, ruler and mat
(optional)

Scissors

THE APPLIQUÉ SKIRT is a knee-length design that features a contrasting lower skirt section. I chose to make this particular skirt from linen for its unique texture. The ruching adds an element of whimsy and the sequins bring a little extra sparkle.

MY INITIAL SKETCH

I'd originally planned to include a floral appliqué design, but I found the abstract swirl of the design more appealing, and the sequins added the perfect sparkle. This skirt looks fabulous when paired with the Parisian Jacket (page 128).

37

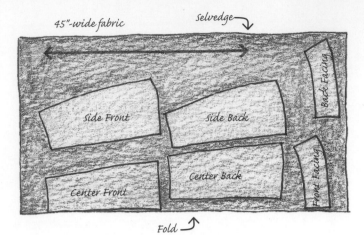

45"-wide fabric

Selvedge

Side Front

Side Back

Back Facing

Center Front

Center Back

Front Facing

Fold

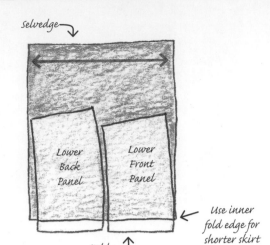

Selvedge

Lower Back Panel

Lower Front Panel

Use inner fold edge for shorter skirt

Fold

60"-wide fabric

Center Front

Side Front

Center Back

Fold of fabric

Front Facing

Back Facing

Side Back

Selvedge

Fold

Lower Back Panel

Lower Front Pane;

Fold

Selvage

Scant ¼" seam allowance

FIGURE 1

38

LAYOUT

Because I used linen to create this skirt, I've included an illustration showing pattern placement for 60"-wide fabric, a width typical for linens. From the tissue pattern, use the cutting line for the knee-length skirt. Cut Center Front, Center Back, Side Front, Side Back, and Facings from the main fabric. Cut the Lower Front and the Lower Back from contrast fabric placed on the fold. The illustration for the 45"-wide fabric shows how to place the pieces if you're using fabric with a directional print. If there is no apparent direction to the print, then lay the pieces out however best conserves fabric, making sure to follow the grainline.

CONSTRUCTION

1. Follow the steps in **General Construction**, skipping the section for the pocket. Continue with *Sew the Skirt Sections and Add the Zipper* through the *Hem the Skirt* section.

2. Once the skirt has been hemmed, edgestitch along the pressed bottom edge of the skirt.

3. To add the ruching, cut one strip about 2" wide from 60"-wide fabric, or two from 45"-wide fabric. Using a ¼" seam allowance, sew the short ends, right sides together, to form one long strip. Press the seam open.

4. Fold the strip in half lengthwise, right sides together, matching the raw edges. Stitch a scant ¼" seam down the length of the strip, forming a long tube. (figure 1)

5. Turn the tube right side out and press, centering the seam along the back side.

6. Thread a hand needle with matching thread and knot the ends together. (figure 2)

7. Begin at one end of the pressed fabric strip and create a series of long running stitches in a zigzag pattern, stitching off the edge on each side. (figure 3)

8. After sewing a few inches of stitches, pull the thread to cause the strip to gather up. It will resemble rickrack. (figure 4) Continue in this manner, stitching and pulling the thread every few inches until the entire strip has been ruched.

9. After ruching the entire strip, measure to make sure you have about 1 yard of trim. Make a few smaller stitches at the end to secure the stitching, then clip the threads.

10. Arrange the ruching along the left front side seam in random loops and curves (refer to project photo), pinning as you go. Extend the ruching into the lower section of the skirt slightly. (figure 5)

11. Once the entire strip has been pinned, turn each end under by ¼" so the ends are finished.

12. Sew through the center of the ruching using a straight machine stitch, following the curves and loops.

13. Add sequins as desired, hand-stitching them to the ruching and surrounding fabric. If you do add sequins, use caution when ironing the skirt, as the sequins can be damaged by the heat.

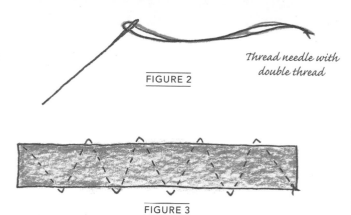

Thread needle with double thread

FIGURE 2

FIGURE 3

Strip resembles rickrack when stitches are pulled

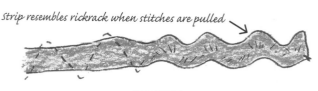

FIGURE 4

Ruching strip

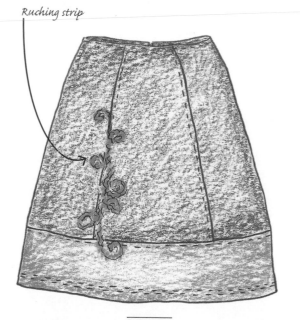

FIGURE 5

make it your own

You can easily change the appliqué for this skirt by cutting a floral shape from contrast fabric and sewing it on, or using a pre-made appliqué. Decorative buttons would also be a nice touch, or some pretty ribbon in a loop-and-curve pattern.

Skirts

TAILORED SKIRT

Materials list

Main Fabric:

All sizes: 1½ yards

Contrast Fabric:

All sizes: ½ yard

Yardages for all fabrics based on 45"-wide cotton fabric

Other Supplies

¼ yard of 20"-wide fusible interfacing for light- to medium-weight fabrics

9" invisible zipper

Polyester machine thread to match fabrics

Rotary cutter, ruler and mat (optional)

Scissors

THE TAILORED SKIRT is a knee-length design that features two pockets with contrast fabric and prominent topstitched seams. The contrast fabric is also featured between the seams at the side front and back as well as the lower edge of the skirt. I chose a bold floral for this skirt with a coordinating trim so that the details would stand out from the print and highlight the stitching. This skirt would also be nice in a textured fabric such as linen with silk accents.

MY INITIAL SKETCH

The original sketch reflects a simple tailored design. I often let fabric speak to me, so when I found the brown and gray fabric, I altered the design to include the trim on the pockets, hem and between the panels.

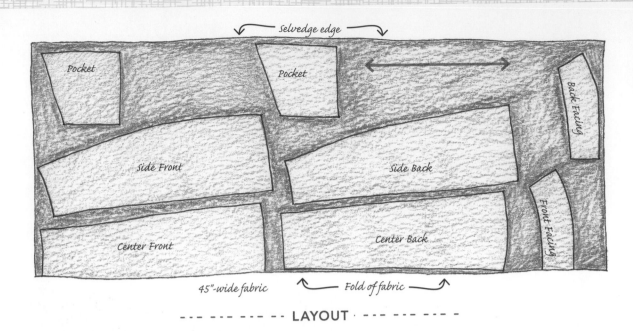

Selvedge edge

Pocket

Pocket

Back Facing

Side Front

Side Back

Front Facing

Center Front

Center Back

45"-wide fabric

Fold of fabric

LAYOUT

From the tissue pattern, use the at-knee length skirt without the lower panel cutting line. Cut Center Front, Center Back, Side Fronts, Side Backs, Facings and four Pocket pieces from the main fabric. The layout above shows how to place the pieces if you're using fabric with a directional print. If there is no apparent direction to the print, then lay the pieces out however best conserves fabric, making sure to follow the grainline.

CONSTRUCTION

Follow the steps in **General Construction** to *Prepare the Waistline Facing*.

1. Cut seven 2"-wide strips by the width of the fabric from the contrast fabric. Trim away the selvedge edges from the ends. Stitch two of the strips together along the narrow end, right sides together with a ¼" seam allowance. Press the seam open. (Set this pieced strip aside for later use as the hem band).

2. Fold the remaining strips in half lengthwise, wrong sides together, matching the raw edges, and press.

3. Use one strip for the top edge of the pocket and follow the *Make the Pocket* instructions in **General Construction**.

4. To add contrasting trim to the skirt panels, with right sides facing and matching the raw edges, pin one length of contrasting trim to each side of the Center Front piece. Extend the trim at the top and bottom by about ½". For the Center Back pieces, pin the contrasting trim to the left side of the left Center Back piece, and the right side of the right Center Back piece. (figure 1) Sew the contrasting trim to all of the skirt pieces with a ¼" seam.

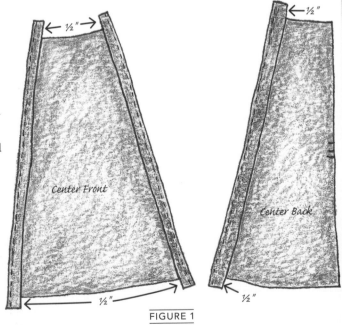

Center Front

Center Back

½"

½"

½"

½"

FIGURE 1

5. Continue with the instructions in **General Construction** for *Sew the Skirt Sections and Add the Zipper*. Press the contrasting trim toward the Side Front and Side Back pieces. Edgestitch along the seams as directed. (figure 2)

6. Complete *Sew the Side Seams and Add the Facings* section in **General Construction**. Also complete a third line of stitching at the waistline, ¼" below the second line of topstitching. (figure 3)

- - - - - - - - - HEM BAND - - - - - - - - -

1. For the hem band, use the remaining long strip of contrasting fabric. Unfold one end and press ½" in to the wrong side. (figure 4) Refold.

2. With right sides together and matching the raw edges, starting at the center seam on the skirt's back, pin the hem band to the lower edge of the skirt. Using a ¼" seam allowance, begin stitching approximately 2" away from the center seam. Stitch all the way around, stopping 2" before the center seam. (figure 5)

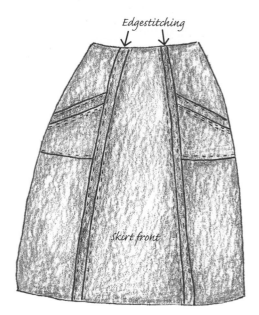

Edgestitching

Skirt front

FIGURE 2

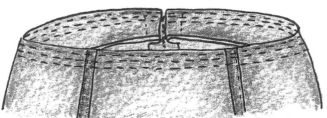

Topstitching detail at waistline

FIGURE 3

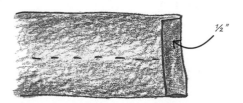

½"

FIGURE 4

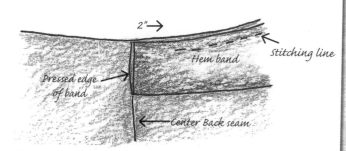

2"

stitching line

Hem band

Pressed edge of band

Center Back seam

FIGURE 5

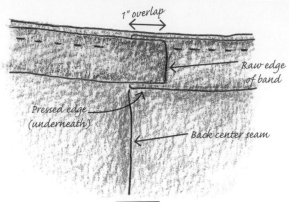

1" overlap

Raw edge of band

Pressed edge (underneath)

Back center seam

FIGURE 6

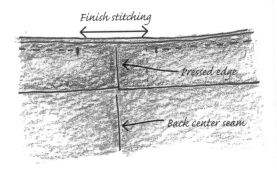

Band, opened up

Pressed edge

Back center seam

Raw edge concealed

FIGURE 7A

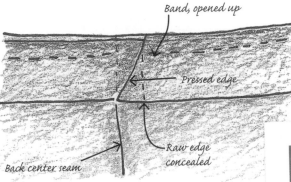

Finish stitching

Pressed edge

Back center seam

FIGURE 7B

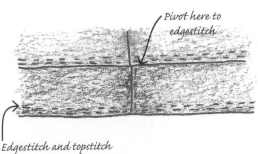

Pivot here to edgestitch

Edgestitch and topstitch along bottom edge

FIGURE 8

3. Overlap the hem band approximately 1" past the pressed end. (figure 6) Trim away any excess.

4. Unfold the pressed end of the band and tuck the raw end inside. Then refold the band and match the raw edges. Finish stitching the band to the bottom edge of the skirt. (figures 7a, 7b)

5. Press the seam toward the top of the skirt. Beginning at the back center seam, edgestitch on the main fabric. Stitch again above that, ¼" away. When the stitching is completed, stitch through the layers where the hem band is joined together to secure the ends. Edgestitch along the bottom folded edge at the contrasting band. Topstitch ¼" away from the edgestitching. (figure 8)

make it your own

Instead of straight stitches, make this skirt unique by adding a decorative stitch as your topstitching. Choose a stitch that will complement the fabric, such as a floral or geometric pattern that mimics the motif in the print. Select a contrasting thread color so that the stitching will show.

MULTI-FABRIC SKIRT

Materials list

For all sizes:

Fabric A (Center Front and Center Back): ¾ yard

Fabric B (Right Side Front and Left Side Back): ¾ yard

Fabric C (Left Side Front and Right Side Back): ¾ yard

Fabric D (Pocket): ¼ yard

Fabric E (Pocket Ruffle and Hem Ruffle): ¼ yard

Yardages for all fabrics based on 45"-wide cotton fabric

Other Supplies

2½ yards of ¾"-wide rickrack trim

¼ yard of 20"-wide fusible interfacing for light- to medium-weight fabrics

9" invisible zipper

Polyester machine thread to match fabrics

Rotary cutter, ruler and mat (optional)

Scissors

Ruffler attachment for sewing machine (optional)

Marking pen or pencil

THE MULTI-FABRIC SKIRT uses a combination of five coordinating fabric prints. Have you ever seen a collection of fabric that you loved so much, you wanted to buy all the pieces? Here's your excuse to buy all of the prints you love, and then put them together in a way that makes the most of them.

MY INITIAL SKETCH

Notice in my original sketch how the pocket was on the right side; I switched it to the left. The sketch also shows a partial ruffle because this is an optional design element. So you be the designer and decide: to ruffle, or not to ruffle?

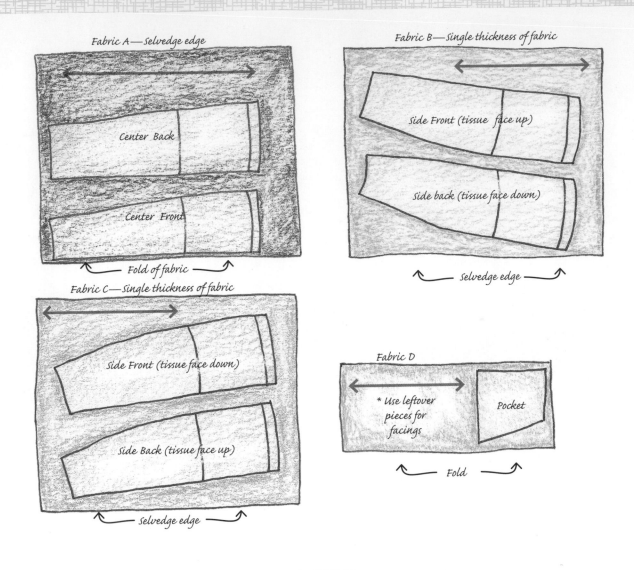

Fabric A—Selvedge edge

Center Back

Center Front

Fold of fabric

Fabric B—Single thickness of fabric

Side Front (tissue face up)

Side back (tissue face down)

selvedge edge

Fabric C—Single thickness of fabric

Side Front (tissue face down)

Side Back (tissue face up)

selvedge edge

Fabric D

* Use leftover pieces for facings

Pocket

Fold

LAYOUT

From the tissue pattern, use the cutting lines from the full-length skirt. The layouts above show flipped tissue pattern pieces; this allows you to correctly cut both the left and right sides of the Side Front and Side Back pieces of the skirt. The layout also shows how to place the pieces if you're using fabric with a directional print. If there is no apparent direction to the print, then lay the pieces out however best conserves fabric, making sure to follow the grainline. The facings are *not* shown, but can be cut from Fabric D.

CONSTRUCTION

Follow the steps in **General Construction** for *Prepare the Waistline Facing.*

CONTRAST FOR POCKET

1. Cut two 2"-wide strips by the width of fabric from Fabric E. Trim selvedge edges from the ends. Allowing a ¼" seam, piece the two strips, right sides together, along one of the narrow ends, making one long strip.

2. Press the seam open. Fold the strip in half lengthwise with the wrong sides together, matching the raw edges, and press.

3. Use a long, straight stitch to sew two rows at ¼" and ⅜" from the raw edges. Create gathers by pulling on the bobbin threads. Or use a ruffler attachment to gather at every 6th stitch, sewing along the length of the raw edges approximately ⅜" from the edge. Press flat.

4. With right sides together and matching the raw edges, stitch the ruffle to one of the Pocket pieces at the top and bottom edges. Follow the *Make the Pocket* instructions in **General Construction** to complete the pocket and its placement on the left Side Front. (figure 1)

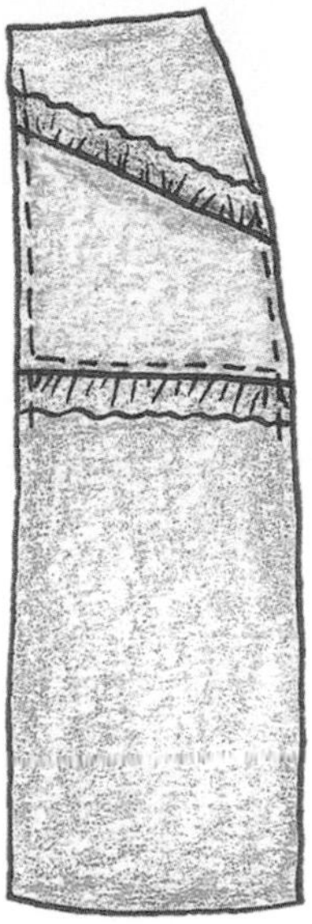

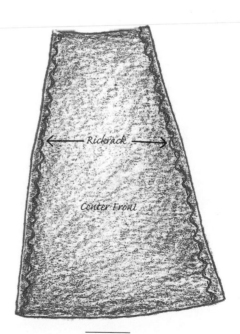

FIGURE 1

ADDING RICKRACK TRIM FOR SIDE FRONT AND BACK

1. Pin the rickrack trim to the sides of the Center Front and Center Back pieces along the ½" seam allowance. Sew down the middle of the trim. (figure 2)

2. Continue with the *Sew the Skirt Sections and Add the Zipper* instructions in **General Construction**, except that you press the Center Front and Center Back seams toward the Side pieces so that the rickrack trim lies on top of the Center Front and Center Back. Edgestitch and topstitch the seams. (figure 3)

3. Complete *Sew the Side Seams and Add the Facings* section in **General Construction**.

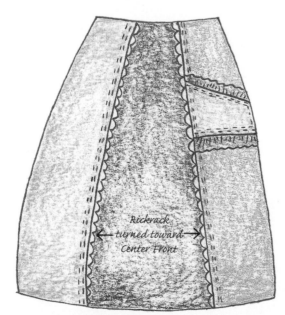

FIGURE 3

FIGURE 2

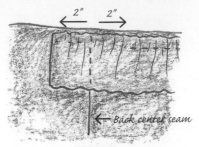

2" 2"

← Back center seam

FIGURE 4

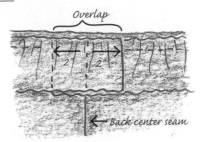

Overlap

2" 2"

← Back center seam

FIGURE 5

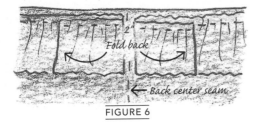

2"

Fold back

← Back center seam

FIGURE 6

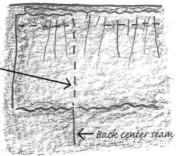

Draw line down pressed crease

← Back center seam

FIGURE 7

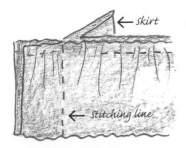

← skirt

← stitching line

FIGURE 8

- - - - - - - RUFFLE HEM - - - - - - -

1. For the ruffle hem, cut two 4"-wide strips from Fabric E by the width of fabric. Trim off the selvedge edges from each end. Allowing a ¼" seam, piece the two strips, right sides together, along one of the narrow ends, making one long strip. Press the seam allowance open.

2. Fold the strip in half lengthwise, wrong sides together, and press.

3. Use a long, straight stitch to sew two rows at ¼" and ⅜" from the raw edges. Create gathers by pulling on the bobbin threads. Or use a ruffler attachment to gather at every 6th stitch, sewing along the length of the raw edges approximately ⅜" from the edge. Press flat.

4. Pin the ruffle to the right side of the skirt, beginning 2" to the left of the back center seam, adjusting the gathers to fit, aligning the raw edges of the ruffle and skirt. (figure 4)

5. Begin stitching the ruffle in place, starting 2" in from the back center seam, using a ½" seam allowance. Stitch all the way around the hem, stopping 2" before the beginning. (figure 5) Clip the threads.

6. Press both loose ends of the ruffle back on themselves, matching all the raw edges, positioning the folds even with the back center seam. (figure 6) Open the folded ends and draw a line on each pressed crease. (figure 7)

7. Trim the ruffle ends to within 1" of the markings. With right sides together, match the markings and stitch the ruffle ends together. (figure 8)

8. Stitch again in the seam allowance to reinforce the seam, approximately ⅛" away from the original stitching. Trim the seam, then press to the side.

9. Pin the open area of the ruffle to the skirt, matching the seam with the back center seam and stitch in place.

10. Serge, or trim and finish the seam edge with a zigzag stitch. Press the seam toward the skirt.

11. Topstitch the skirt close to the seamline. Repeat ¼" away from the first row of stitching.

make it your own

To make this skirt your own, how about choosing a different trim between the Side Front and Side Back? Or you could buy an additional fabric for a contrasting strip between the seams, like the Tailored Skirt. Another option—which I like—would be to add a sweet appliqué to the pocket.

THREE-FABRIC SKIRT

Materials list

For all sizes:

Fabric A (all main skirt pieces and facings): 1⅝ yards

Fabric B (pockets and part of ruffle): ⅔ yard

Fabric C (contrast for pocket and ruffle): ⅓ yard

Yardages for all fabrics based on 45"-wide cotton fabric

Other Supplies

¼ yard 20"-wide fusible interfacing for light- to medium-weight fabrics

9" invisible zipper

Polyester machine thread to match fabrics

Rotary cutter, ruler and mat (optional)

Ruffler attachment for sewing machine (optional)

Scissors

THE THREE-FABRIC SKIRT is designed to fall just below the knee. It features two ruffle-trimmed pockets and showcases one prominent print, with two coordinates for the pockets and ruffles. It's a great way to use three wonderful, bold prints. Black-and-white fabrics or bold geometric prints would work well for this skirt.

MY INITIAL SKETCH

This original sketch shows how coordinating fabrics with very different motifs can blend nicely, adding texture and punch. Using lots of prints from a line of fabrics is one of my favorite techniques. Maybe that's because I don't fall in love with an individual fabric—I fall in love with the entire line!

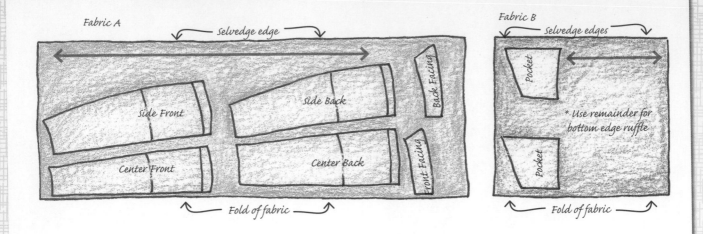

Fabric A
Selvedge edge
Side Front
Center Front
Side Back
Center Back
Back Facing
Front Facing
Fold of fabric

Fabric B
Selvedge edges
Pocket
Pocket
*Use remainder for bottom edge ruffle
Fold of fabric

LAYOUT

From the tissue pattern, use the cutting lines for the full-length skirt. Cut four Pocket pieces from Fabric B. The remaining portion of Fabric B will be cut into strips for the lower ruffle. The layout also shows how to place the pieces if you're using fabric with a directional print. If there is no apparent direction to the print, then lay the pieces out however best conserves fabric, making sure to follow the grainline.

CONSTRUCTION

Follow the steps in **General Construction** for *Prepare the Waistline Facing.*

CONTRAST FOR POCKET

1. Cut two 2"-wide strips by the width of fabric from Fabric C. Trim the selvedge edges from the ends and piece the two strips, right sides together, along one of the narrow ends with a ¼" seam, making one long strip.

2. Press the seam open. Fold the strip in half lengthwise with wrong sides together and press.

3. Use a long, straight stitch to sew two rows, one at ¼" and one at ⅜" from the raw edges. Create gathers by pulling on the bobbin threads. Or use a ruffler attachment to gather at every 6th stitch, sewing along the length of the raw edges approximately ⅜" from the edge. Press flat.

4. With right sides together, matching the raw edges, stitch the ruffle to both of the Pocket pieces at the top and bottom edges. Follow the *Make the Pocket* instructions in **General Construction** to complete the pockets. (figure 1)

Side Front: right

Side Front: left

FIGURE 1

- - - SEWING THE SKIRT TOGETHER - - -

Complete *Sew the Skirt Sections and Add the Zipper* and *Sew the Side Seams and Add the Facings* sections of the **General Construction**.

- - - - - - - - RUFFLE HEM - - - - - - - - -

1. For the ruffle hem, cut four 3¼"-wide strips by the width of fabric from Fabric B and two 3"-wide strips by the width of fabric from Fabric C. Trim off the selvedge edges from each end.

2. Match two short ends of the Fabric B strips, right sides together, and stitch with a ¼" seam allowance. Press the seam open. Repeat for the two remaining Fabric B strips. Piece the Fabric C strips together the same way. There should now be three long strips all approximately the same length. (figure 2)

3. Place the Fabric C strip against one of the Fabric B strips, right sides together, matching the raw edges on the long sides, and sew together with a ¼" seam. (figure 3a). Press the seam to one side.

4. Sew the remaining Fabric B strip to the other side of the Fabric C strip in the same manner, pressing the seam to one side. (figure 3b)

5. Fold the strip unit in half lengthwise, wrong sides together, and press. Half of the Fabric C strip will show on the front, and the other half will show on the back. (figure 4)

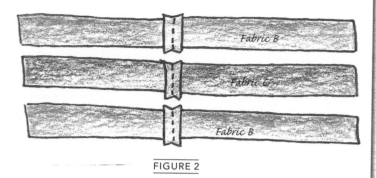

Fabric B

Fabric C

Fabric B

FIGURE 2

Fabric B

Fabric C

FIGURE 3A

strips after being sewn together

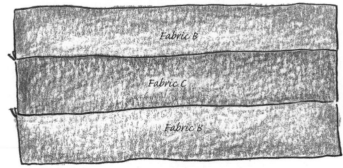

Fabric B

Fabric C

Fabric B

FIGURE 3B

Fabric B

Fabric C—half showing on each side

FIGURE 4

55

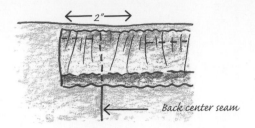

FIGURE 5

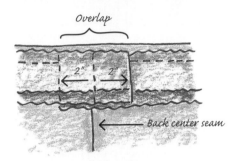

FIGURE 6

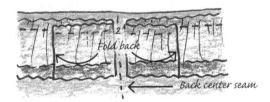

FIGURE 7A

Draw line down pressed crease

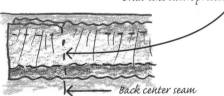

FIGURE 7B

6. Use a long, straight stitch to sew two rows, one at ¼" and one at ⅜" from the raw edges. Create gathers by pulling on the bobbin threads. Or use a ruffler attachment to gather at every 6th stitch, sewing along the length of the raw edges approximately ⅜" from the edge. Press flat.

7. Pin the ruffle to the right side of the skirt, beginning 2" to the left of the back center seam. Adjust the gathers to fit, aligning the raw edges of the ruffle and skirt. (figure 5)

8. Begin stitching the ruffle in place, starting 2" away from the back center seam, using a ½" seam allowance. Stitch all the way around the hem, stopping 2" before the back center seam. (figure 6) Clip the threads.

9. Press both loose ends of the ruffle back on themselves, matching all the raw edges, positioning the folds even with the back center seam. Open out the folded ends and draw a line on each pressed crease. (figures 7a, 7b)

10. Trim the ruffle ends to within 1" of the markings. With right sides together, match the markings and stitch the ruffle ends together. (figure 8)

11. Stitch again in the seam allowance to reinforce the seam, approximately ⅛" away from the original stitching. Trim the seam down, and press to one side.

12. Pin the open area of the ruffle to the skirt, matching the ruffle seam with the back center seam. Stitch in place.

13. Serge, or trim and finish the seam edge with a zigzag stitch. Press the seam toward the skirt.

14. Topstitch the skirt close to the seamline. Repeat topstitching ¼" away from the first row of stitching.

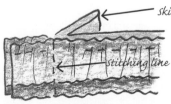

FIGURE 8

make it your own

Add your own style by changing up the way the ruffle is made; try cutting it a different width or leave out the contrast through the center of it. Another idea is to include the contrast ruffle only at the top of the pocket, or just at the bottom. Go for a more tailored look by making the contrast a plain band instead of a ruffle.

RUFFLED SKIRT

Materials list

Main Fabric (all main skirt
pieces and facings):
All sizes: 1⅝ yards
(45"-wide fabric)
Contrast Fabric (lower band):
All sizes: ½ yard
(45"-wide fabric)
Ruffle Contrast Fabric
All sizes: ⅔ yard (54"-wide
fabric) or 1 yard (45"-
wide fabric)

Other Supplies

¼ yard of 20"-wide fusible
interfacing for light- to
medium-weight fabrics
9" invisible zipper
Polyester machine thread to
match fabrics
Rotary cutter, ruler and mat
(optional)
Scissors
Ruffler attachment for
sewing machine (optional)

THE RUFFLED SKIRT hits at mid-calf, and has a band of contrasting fabric at the bottom. I chose a large-scale floral print with a bold geometric contrast fabric. This creates the perfect background for the other contrast fabric: the silk ruffle. A silk rose embellishes the lower band's seamline.

When choosing fabric for this skirt, pick fabrics that have a strong contrast. The silk provides a lovely textural difference, but a third contrasting fabric of any kind would work for this design.

MY INITIAL SKETCH

For this skirt, I envisioned using two cottons and a silk. The texture of the silk gives the skirt a luxurious look, and the addition of the silk rose brings it all together. This skirt pairs wonderfully with the Silk and Linen jacket (page 122).

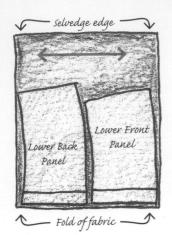

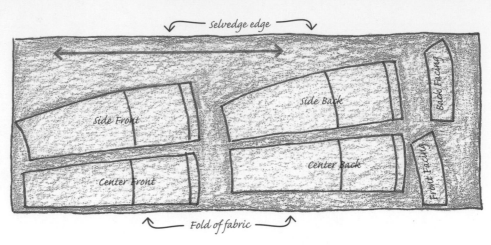

selvedge edge

Lower Back Panel

Lower Front Panel

Side Front

Center Front

Side Back

Center Back

Back Facing

Front Facing

Fold of fabric

selvedge edge

Fold of fabric

LAYOUT

From the tissue pattern, use the cutting lines from the full-length skirt. Cut all main skirt pieces from the main fabric and the lower band from the contrast fabric. The layout shows how to place the pieces if you're using fabric with a directional print. If there is no apparent direction to the print, then lay the pieces out however best conserves fabric, making sure to follow the grainline.

CONSTRUCTION

Follow the steps in **General Construction** for *Prepare the Waistline Facing.*

ADD CONTRAST RUFFLE TRIM AND SEW THE SKIRT TOGETHER

1. Cut four 2½" strips by the width of the fabric from the ruffle contrast fabric. Trim away the selvedge edges from the ends.

2. Fold all strips in half lengthwise, wrong sides together, and press.

3. Use a long, straight stitch to complete two rows of stitching from the raw edges, one at ¼" and one at ⅜". Create gathers by pulling on the bobbin threads. Or use a ruffler attachment to gather at every 6th stitch, sewing along the length of the raw edges approximately ⅜" from the edge. Press flat.

4. To add the contrasting ruffle trim to the skirt panels, pin one ruffle along each of the Center Front side seams, matching all the raw edges. Adjust the gathers so the ruffle extends about ½" beyond the edge at the top and bottom of the Center Front. Repeat along the sides of the Center Back pieces. (figure 1)

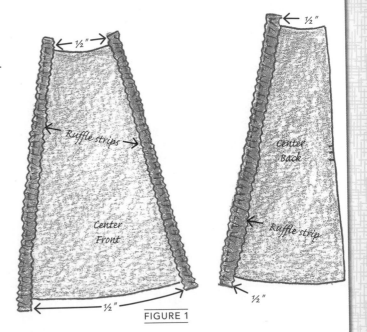

Ruffle strips

Center Front

Center Back

Ruffle strip

½"

½"

½"

½"

FIGURE 1

5. Sew the ruffle trim to the skirt pieces with a ⅜" seam.

6. Continue with the instructions in **General Construction** for *Sew the Skirt Sections and Add the Zipper*, with the following exceptions: Press the ruffle trim toward the Side Front and Side Back. Press the side seams toward the Center Front and Center Back. Edgestitch along the seams as directed. (figure 2)

7. Complete the *Sew the Side Seams and Add the Facings* section in **General Construction**.

ADD CONTRAST RUFFLE TRIM FOR LOWER SKIRT AND HEM

1. Cut two 3"-wide strips (for 54" width fabric) or three 3"-wide strips (for 45" width fabric) by the width of the fabric from ruffle contrast fabric. Trim off the selvedge edges. Matching the short ends, sew the two 54"-wide or three 45"-wide strips, right sides together, with a ¼" seam allowance to make a long strip. This will be the ruffle between the lower skirt and main skirt. Press all seams open.

2. Fold the strip in half lengthwise, wrong sides together, and press.

3. Use a long, straight stitch to complete two rows of stitching, one at ¼" and one at ⅜" from the raw edges. Create gathers by pulling on the bobbin threads. Or use a ruffler attachment to gather at every 6th stitch, sewing along the length of the raw edges approximately ⅜" from the edge. Press flat.

4. Pin the ruffle to the right side of the skirt, beginning 2" to the left of the back center seam, adjusting the gathers to fit, aligning the raw edges of the ruffle and skirt. (figure 3)

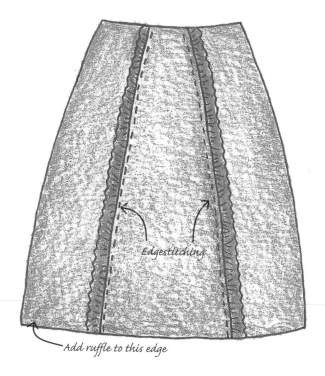

Edgestitching

Add ruffle to this edge

FIGURE 2

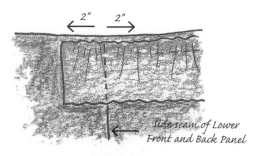

2"　2"

Side seam of Lower Front and Back Panel

FIGURE 3

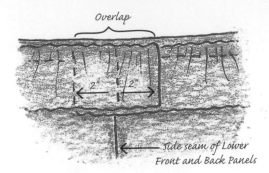

Overlap

2" 2"

Side seam of Lower
Front and Back Panels

FIGURE 4

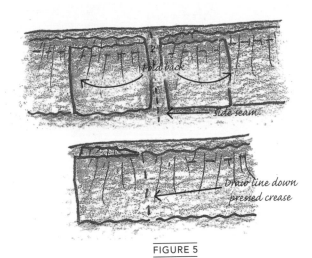

2"
Fold back

Side seam

Draw line down
pressed crease

FIGURE 5

5. Begin stitching the ruffle in place, starting 2" in from the back center seam, using a ½" seam allowance. Stitch all the way around the main skirt, stopping 2" from the back center seam. (figure 4) Clip the threads.

6. Press both loose ends of the ruffle back on themselves, matching all the raw edges, positioning the folds even with the back center seam. Open out the folded ends and draw a line on each pressed crease. (figure 5)

7. Trim the ruffle ends to within 1" of the markings, with right sides together, matching up the markings and stitch the ruffle ends together. (figure 6)

8. Stitch again in the seam allowance to reinforce the seam, approximately ⅛" away from the original stitching. Trim the seam down and press to one side.

9. Pin the open area of the ruffle to the skirt, matching the seam with the back center seam. Stitch in place.

10. Follow the instructions for the *Add the Lower Skirt* in **General Construction**.

11. To add the ruffle hem to the bottom edge of the skirt, repeat steps 1 through 9, except cut the ruffle trim 4" wide.

12. Press the seam toward the lower skirt panel and edgestitch close to the seamline.

- - - - - - - - - - **FLOWER** - - - - - - - -

1. To make the flower, cut one 2"-wide strip by the width of the fabric from the ruffle contrast fabric.

2. Fold in half lengthwise, wrong sides together, with the raw edges even, and press.

3. Use a long, straight stitch to sew two rows of stitching, one at ¼" and one at ⅜" from the raw edge. Create gathers by pulling on the bobbin threads. Or use a ruffler attachment set to gather at every stitch sewing approximately ¼" from the long raw edge.

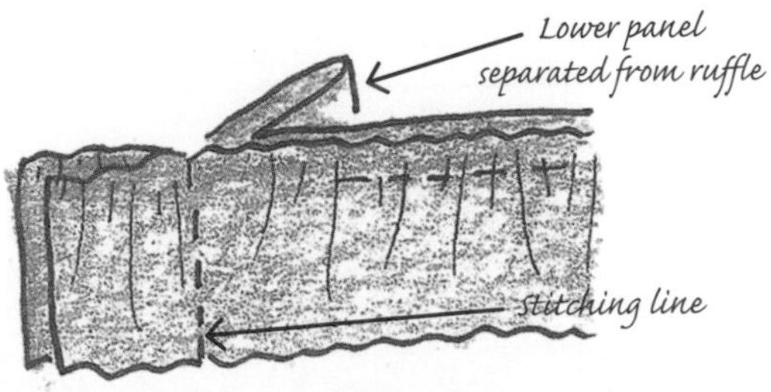

Lower panel
separated from ruffle

stitching line

FIGURE 6

4. Thread a hand-sewing needle with matching thread and knot. Fold down the corner of one end of the strip so that the top corner hits the raw gathered edge. Trim off the fabric extending beyond the raw, gathered edge. (figure 7) Secure with needle and thread.

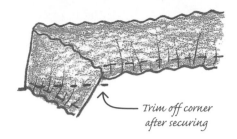

Trim off corner after securing

FIGURE 7

5. Roll up the strip, taking stitches along the raw edge as needed to secure the layers. Finish by turning the remaining end in diagonally toward the inside of the flower so that the top corner hits the raw, gathered edge. (Don't feel like you must use the full length of the strip; make the flower as large or small as you wish.) Trim off the excess fabric and stitch in place. (figure 8)

6. Stitch or pin the flower to the lower left side front seam where the lower skirt panel meets the main skirt.

Trim off remaining corner after securing

FIGURE 8

working with silk

If you decide to work with silk, be aware that it loves to fray! Whenever I create a silk ruffle strip, I serge the edge before gathering it to keep it tamed. If you decide to serge the edge, be careful not to remove any fabric width! Just serge the edge to finish it off. If you don't own a serger, use your sewing machine's zigzag or overlock stitch.

make it your own

Change where the silk is used on this skirt. Try making it the lower portion instead of a contrasting trim; just switch the yardage requirements around. If you like, you can also add a pocket or two to this skirt by following the instructions from one of the other variations. The skirt could also be made all from one fabric for a different look. Just add the yardage requirements together.

Materials list

Main Fabric (all main skirt
pieces and facings)

All sizes: 1⅝ yards

Contrast Fabric (lower band)

All sizes: ⅔ yard

Tie Fabric

All sizes: ⅛ yard

*Yardages for all fabrics based on
45"-wide cotton fabric*

Other Supplies

¼ yard of 20"-wide fusible
interfacing for light- to
mid-weight fabrics

9" invisible zipper

Polyester machine thread to
match fabrics

Rotary cutter, ruler and mat
(optional)

Scissors

Ruffler attachment for
sewing machine (optional)

Chalk pencil

THE FLORAL SKIRT is mid-calf length with a large ruffle at the lower edge made from contrasting fabric. A delicate little tie of a third contrasting fabric is added between the skirt and ruffle for subtle detailing. This skirt is the perfect canvas for a very large-scale floral print. I chose to carefully offset the motif on the center front for interest. Watch your layout if using a fabric with this characteristic so you can capture its best features.

MY INITIAL SKETCH

The original sketch here reflects the soft, feminine look I wanted. After sewing it together, though, I decided it needed a bit more embellishment, so I added a pretty tie in a contrasting fabric.

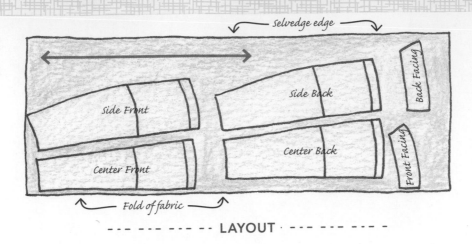

selvedge edge

Side Front

Center Front

Side Back

Center Back

Back Facing

Front Facing

Fold of fabric

LAYOUT

From the tissue pattern, use the cutting lines for the full-length skirt. Cut all main skirt pieces from the main fabric. The layout shows how to place the pieces if you're using fabric with a directional print. If there is no apparent direction to the print, then lay the pieces out however best conserves fabric, making sure to follow the grainline. If you're using a fabric with a large motif, move around the tissue pattern to determine how you should layout the pattern pieces to maximize the impact of the motifs, before cutting the fabric.

CONSTRUCTION

Follow the steps in **General Construction** f*or Prepare the Waistline Facing.* Skip the instructions for the pocket and complete *Sew the Skirt Sections and Add the Zipper* as well as *Sew the Side Seams and Add the Facings.*

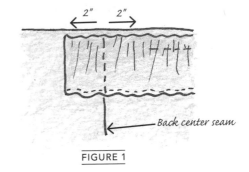

2" 2"

Back center seam

FIGURE 1

RUFFLE

1. Cut two 10"-wide strips by the width of fabric from the contrast fabric. Piece these strips, right sides together, along the 10" edge with a ¼" seam allowance, making one long strip. Serge or clean finish the seam and press it to one side.

2. Use a long, straight stitch to sew two rows of stitching, one at ¼" and one at ⅜" from the raw edges. Create gathers by pulling on the bobbin threads to gather the fabric. Or use a ruffler attachment to gather at every 6th stitch, sewing along the length of the raw edges approximately ⅜" from the edge. Press flat.

3. Pin the ruffle to the skirt, right sides together, starting 2" to the left of the back center seam. Adjust the gathers to fit, aligning the gathered edge of the ruffle with the raw edge of the skirt. (figure 1)

4. Begin stitching the ruffle in place, starting 2" from the back center seam and using a ½" seam allowance. Stitch all the way around the edge of the skirt, stopping 2" before the back center seam. (figure 2) Clip the threads.

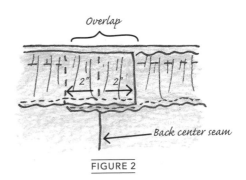

Overlap

2" 2"

Back center seam

FIGURE 2

5. Press both ends of the ruffle back on themselves, matching all the raw edges, positioning the folds even with the back center seam. (figure 3a) Open out the folded ends and draw a line on each pressed crease. (figure 3b)

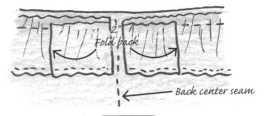

FIGURE 3A

6. Trim away the ruffle ends to within 1" of the markings. With right sides together, match up the markings and stitch the ruffle ends together. (figure 4)

7. Stitch again in the seam allowance to reinforce the seam, approximately ⅛" away from the original stitching. Press the seam to one side.

8. Pin the open area of the ruffle to the skirt, matching the ruffle seam to the back center seam. Stitch in place.

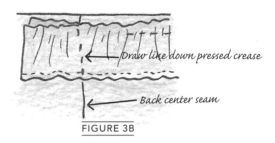

FIGURE 3B

9. Open the ruffle from the skirt and press the seam up.

10. Follow the instructions in **General Construction** for *Hem the Skirt*. Topstitch the hem in place as directed ¾" from the pressed edge. Eliminate the second row of topstitching but edgestitch along the pressed edge.

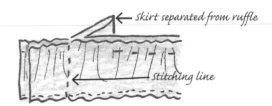

FIGURE 4

- - - - - - - - - - - TIE TRIM - - - - - - - - - -

1. For the tie trim between the skirt and ruffle, cut two 2"-wide strips by the width of the tie fabric. Trim off the selvedge edges and piece the narrow ends, right sides together, with a ¼" seam. Press the seam open.

2. Fold the strip in half lengthwise, right sides together, and stitch along the long edge with a ¼" seam allowance, forming a long tube.

3. Turn the tube right-side out and press with the seam along one edge.

4. To determine where the bow will be, lay the tie along the bottom of the main skirt, with the tie's seam pointing downward. (figure 5) I've positioned the tie so the ends cross at the seam where the left Side Front and Center Front are joined.

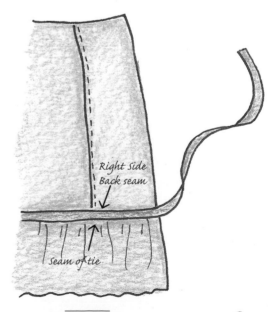

FIGURE 5

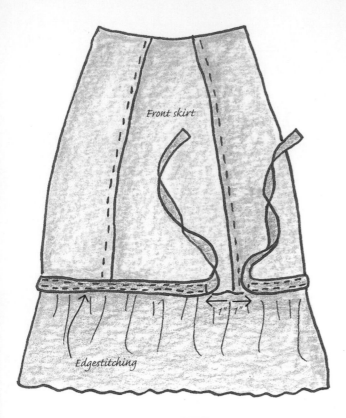

Front skirt

Edgestitching

1" 1"

FIGURE 6

5. Once you're satisfied with the position, pin the tie trim in place with the lower edge just covering the main skirt/ruffle seam. Continue pinning the tie in place around the skirt. Stop within 1" of the seam where the ties will cross to form the bow (here, the left Side Front and Center Front).

6. Edgestitch the upper edge of the tie, starting 1" away from the left Side Front and Center Front and continuing around until you reach the other 1" point. Pivot and sew across the tie, then pivot once more and continue edgestitching, this time along the bottom edge of the tie. When you reach the other side, pivot and stitch across the remaining end of the tie. (figure 6)

7. Tie a bow with the loose ends. Trim off any extra that extends below the hem of the skirt. Untie the bow and turn the raw edges of the tie ends in ¼" and press. (figure 7)

8. Edgestitch the loose ends of the tie trim, starting close to the skirt itself. Pivot at the corners, sew across the end, and continue up the other side, stopping when the skirt is reached. Repeat for the other end of the tie. (figure 8)

9. Tie a bow with the loose ends and gently press flat for a crisp finish.

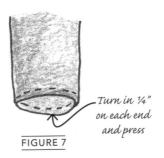

Turn in ¼" on each end and press

FIGURE 7

Begin stitching close to skirt and edgestitch all free edges of ties

FIGURE 8

make it your own

Be creative! Make this skirt unique by changing up the way the fabrics are used. You can create the entire skirt from one fabric by adding up the two yardage requirements. Sewing a fabric flower just above the bow would add a nice touch. The tie would be fabulous made from hand-dyed silk or a velvet ribbon.

Chapter Two

TUNICS AND DRESSES

THE IDEA THAT A tunic can also become a dress is based on my love of a versatile design with simple lines that is easy to sew and compliments anyone. Nothing is better than mastering one pattern that can serve so many purposes! All six projects in this section originate from one basic set of pattern pieces that features details such as a raglan sleeve, Empire waistline, and a closely fitting A-line skirt in three lengths.

The following projects detail six variations: two hip-length tunics that can be worn with a slim skirt or pants, two above-knee-length and two below-knee-length dresses. Through the use of various fabric combinations and embellishments, each project showcases its own unique style and yet remains simple to sew using the same pattern pieces again and again. Suggested fabrics for this design include 100% cotton quilting fabrics, linen or silk.

Once you have mocked up this design following the recommendations in Custom Fitting, you will have a pattern design that is perfect for you. Now it's time to have fun with all of those fabulous fabrics!

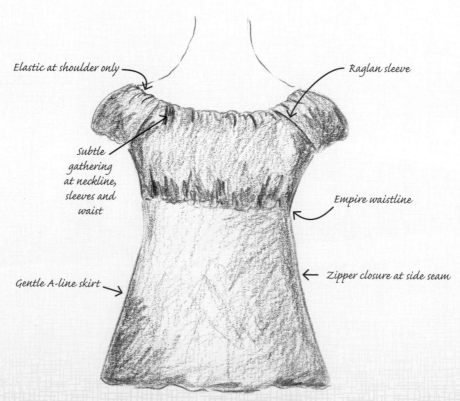

Elastic at shoulder only

Raglan sleeve

Subtle gathering at neckline, sleeves and waist

Empire waistline

Gentle A-line skirt

Zipper closure at side seam

Hip, above-knee or below-knee lengths

GENERAL CONSTRUCTION

Once the fabric pieces have been cut out and all notches have been snipped, remove tissue pattern pieces.

NOTE: All seam allowances are ½" unless otherwise stated.

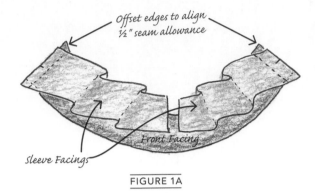

Offset edges to align ½" seam allowance

Sleeve Facings

Front Facing

FIGURE 1A

- - - - - PREPARE THE FACINGS - - - - -

1. Apply fusible interfacing to the wrong sides of Front and Back Facings following the manufacturer's instructions. Note that the Sleeve Facings are *not* backed with interfacing.

2. Matching notches, pin the Sleeve Facings to the Front Facing, right sides together. Offset the edges to align the ½" seam allowance on either side. (figure 1a) Repeat for the Back Facing. (figure 1b)

3. Sew all four seams and press. Finish the outer edge of the facing unit by serging or using a zigzag stitch along the outer edge (figure 2). Set facing unit aside.

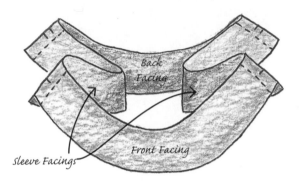

Back Facing

Sleeve Facings

Front Facing

FIGURE 1B

ATTACH THE BODICE AND SKIRT PIECES

1. While the Front and Back Bodices are still folded in half, snip a small triangle from each corner of the fold within the seam allowance. This will mark the center of the neckline as well as at the waistline. (figure 3)

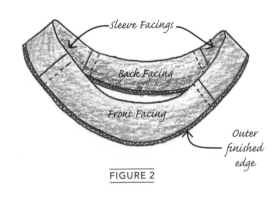

Sleeve Facings

Back Facing

Front Facing

Outer finished edge

FIGURE 2

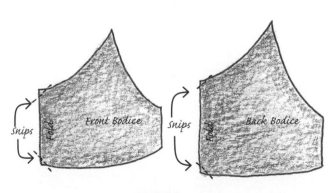

Snips *Fold* *Front Bodice*

Snips *Fold* *Back Bodice*

FIGURE 3

2. Use a long, straight stitch to sew two rows along the lower edge of each Bodice piece, one row at ¼" and the other at ⅜". Begin and end approximately 2" from the side edges. (figure 4)

3. While the Front and Back Skirt are still folded in half, snip away a small triangle from the top edge of the fold to mark the center of each (as you did in step 1 for the bodices).

4. Place the Front Bodice on the Front Skirt, right sides together, matching the center snips. Gently pull the gathering stitches until the lower edge of the bodice is the same size as the top of the skirt. Distribute the gathers evenly and pin in place, keeping the raw edges even. Stitch the bodice to the skirt using a ½" seam allowance. (figure 5). Repeat for the Back Bodice and Back Skirt.

5. Serge the seam or trim the seam and use a zigzag stitch to clean-finish the edge.

6. Press the seam toward the skirt for front and back. Press creases in the bodice pieces to make the gathering lie flat. (See page 21.)

7. Double topstitch close to the seam. (See page 21.) (figure 6)

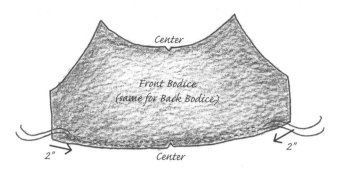

Center

Front Bodice
(same for Back Bodice)

2"   Center   2"

FIGURE 4

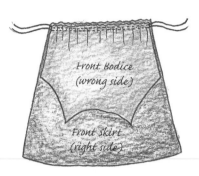

Front Bodice
(wrong side)

Front Skirt
(right side)

FIGURE 5

--- --- · INSTALL THE ZIPPER · -- --- -

1. Clean-finish the edge on the left side of the front and back pieces by serging or using a zigzag stitch. Leave the entire seam allowance open.

2. On the back, mark 3" down from the top on the left side along the finished edge. Repeat for the front piece. (figure 7)

3. Install the invisible zipper. (See page 22.)

4. Once the zipper has been installed, stitch the seam closed above the zipper just like for the seam below the zipper.

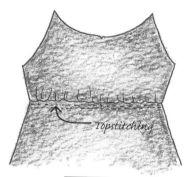

Topstitching

FIGURE 6

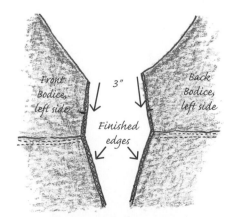

Front
Bodice,
left side

3"

Back
Bodice,
left side

Finished
edges

FIGURE 7

73

5. To reinforce the zipper opening, sew a bartack at the upper edge. Drop the feed dogs on your sewing machine and set it for a tight zigzag that is approximately ⅛" wide. With the zipper closed, center the machine foot over the seam above the zipper as close as possible to the beginning of the zipper opening and stitch. (figure 8)

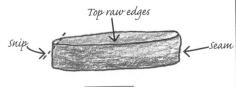

FIGURE 8

SEW THE SIDE SEAM AND SLEEVES

1. Sew the opposite side seam, clean-finishing the edge, and press the seam toward the back.

2. Fold each Sleeve piece in half and snip on the fold within the seam allowance to mark the center.

3. With right sides together, sew the sleeve seam, clean-finish the edge and press.

4. Using the longest straight stitch on your sewing machine, sew two lines of gathering stitches along the bottom edge of each sleeve, ¼" and ⅜" away from the raw edge. Begin and end at the sleeve seam. (figure 9)

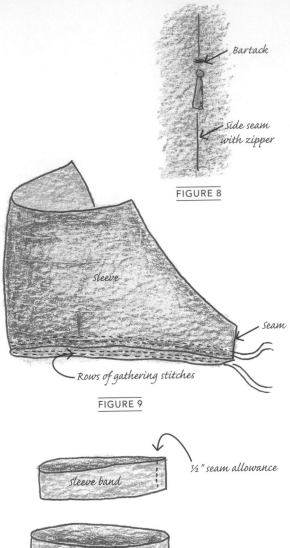

FIGURE 9

5. To make the bands for the sleeves, measure around your upper arm, approximately 3"-4" above the elbow. Add 1½" to this measurement for ease and the seam allowance.

6. Cut two strips from the fabric, 2¼" wide by the measurement determined in the previous step.

7. Sew the narrow ends of each strip together, right sides together, using a ¼" seam allowance. Press the seams to one side. (figure 10)

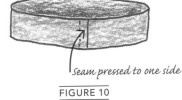

FIGURE 10

8. Fold the bands in half, wrong sides together, with raw edges even and press. With the seam at one end, flatten the band to find the center. Snip a small triangle at the top raw edges to mark the center. (figure 11)

FIGURE 11

sleeve bands

Measuring your arm will result in the best fit for the sleeve band, but, in a pinch, there are some benchmark measurements you can use. (Seam allowances are included.)

XXS: 12¾"	XS: 13"	S: 13¼"	M: 13½"	L: 13¾"	XL: 14"	XXL: 14¼"

9. With right sides together, place the band on the sleeve, matching seams and center snips. Gently pull the gathering stitches until the lower edge of the sleeve is the same size as the band. Distribute the gathers evenly and pin in place, raw edges even. (figure 12)

10. Stitch the band and sleeve together ensuring that the seamline is below the lowest line of gathering stitches. Serge the seam edges or trim and zigzag.

11. Press the seam toward the sleeve. Press creases in the gathering (as you did with the Front and Back Bodice pieces earlier).

12. Edgestitch the sleeve band close to the seam and again along the outer edge. (figure 13)

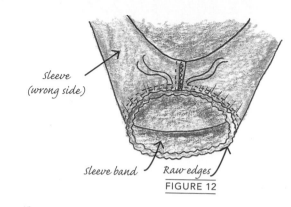

Sleeve (wrong side)

Sleeve band *Raw edges*

FIGURE 12

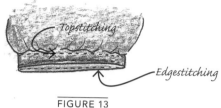

Topstitching

Edgestitching

FIGURE 13

-- ADD THE SLEEVES AND FACINGS --

1. With right sides together, pin the sleeves to the bodice by matching notches and seams. (figure 14)

2. Stitch the seams. Serge the seam or trim the seam and use a zigzag stitch to clean-finish the edge. Press.

3. Fold the Front Facing in half, matching sleeve seams, and snip the center at the fold. Repeat for the Back Facing. (figure 15)

4. Using a long, straight stitch, sew two lines of gathering stitches along the Front and Back Bodice at the neck, ¼" and ⅜" from the raw edges, starting 1½" in from the sleeve seams. (figure 16)

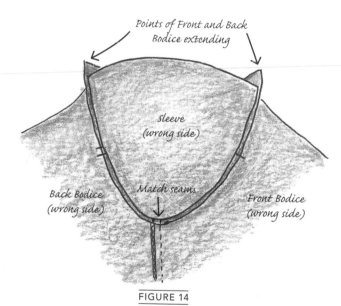

Points of Front and Back Bodice extending

sleeve (wrong side)

Back Bodice (wrong side) *Match seams* *Front Bodice (wrong side)*

FIGURE 14

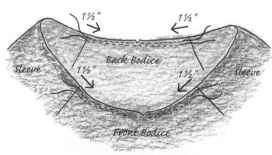

1½" *1½"*

Sleeve *Back Bodice* *Sleeve*

1½" *1½"*

Front Bodice

FIGURE 16

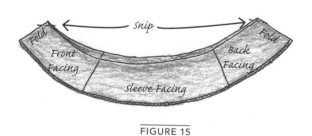

snip

Fold *Fold*

Front Facing *Back Facing*

Sleeve Facing

FIGURE 15

5. Pin the facing unit to the top edge of the bodice and sleeves, right sides together, matching seams and center snips. Gently pull gathering threads until the neckline edges match the facing unit in size. *Note:* Make sure that the larger Front Facing is matched up with the Front Bodice edge before stitching. Sew together with a ½" seam allowance. (figure 17)

6. Trim the seam allowance to ¼" and clip the curve of the neckline over the Sleeve section. On the Front and Back Bodice sections, notch the seam to ease the curve. (figure 18)

7. Understitch the front and back neckline edges as detailed in *Sewing Techniques* (page 25), stopping at the sleeve seams. (The gathering on the sleeves will keep the facings from rolling outward.)

8. Turn the facings to the inside of the bodice and press.

9. To make the casing for the elastic, stitch ½" away from the finished edge along the top of each sleeve. (figure 19)

10. Cut two pieces of elastic ⅜" by 6" long.

11. Secure a small safety pin near one end of the elastic and insert into sleeve casing. Pull the elastic through until only about ½" extends beyond the seam on either side. Pin in place. Repeat for the remaining sleeve. (figure 20)

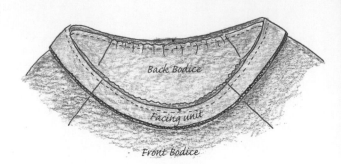

FIGURE 17

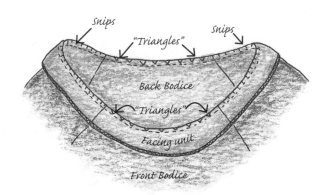

FIGURE 18

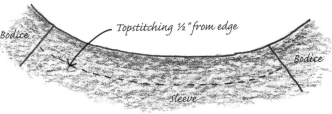

FIGURE 19

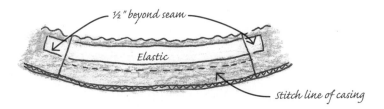

FIGURE 20

76

12. Try on the tunic/dress and check for fit on the neckline. Pull up elastic until you are pleased with the fit. Measure across the top of each sleeve to check that they are the same. Stitch the elastic in place by stitching-in-the-ditch of the sleeve seam on the front and back. Trim the elastic that extends beyond the seamline. (figure 21)

13. Press the entire bodice, intentionally creating creases in the gathering as detailed in the *Sewing Techniques* (page 21). Topstitch around the bodice neckline sections ½" away from the finished edges, matching up with the top of sleeve stitching. Edgestitch the front and back neckline edges to finish. (figure 22)

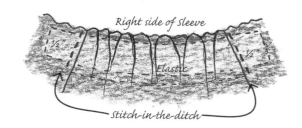

Right side of sleeve

½" ½"

Elastic

stitch-in-the-ditch

FIGURE 21

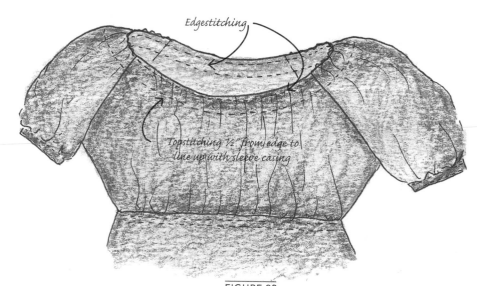

Edgestitching

Topstitching ½" from edge to line up with sleeve casing

FIGURE 22

- - - - - - - - ADD THE HEM - - - - - - - -

1. Serge or zigzag the bottom edge to clean-finish.

2. Turn up 1¼" for the hem and press. Pin in place and topstitch 1" up from pressed edge. Stitch again ¼" away from first line of stitching. Edgestitch along the folded edge of the bottom as desired. (figure 23)

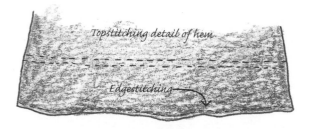

Topstitching detail of hem

Edgestitching

FIGURE 23

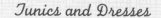

THE DAMASK TUNIC is a classic hip-length design with contrasting accents (the tie belt and bottom hem). It looks great with a slim skirt or pants. The simplicity of this variation showcases the detailing of the fabric design itself. Think large-scale prints or damasks with intricate detailing when choosing fabrics for the Damask Tunic.

Materials list

Main Fabric:

Sizes XXS–L: 2¼ yards

Sizes XL–XXL: 2¾ yards

Contrast Fabric for tie belt, sleeve and bottom band:

All Sizes: ⅔ yard

Yardages for all fabrics based on 45"-wide cotton fabric

Other Supplies

¼ yard of 20"-wide fusible interfacing for light- to medium-weight fabrics

14" invisible zipper

Polyester machine thread to match fabrics

Rotary cutter, ruler and mat (optional)

Scissors

½ yard of ⅜"-wide elastic

Chalk pencil

MY INITIAL SKETCH

I originally envisioned a simple tunic with a tie belt. Once I sewed it up, I decided it needed a little something extra, so I added the hem band. It turned out to create an even more polished look!

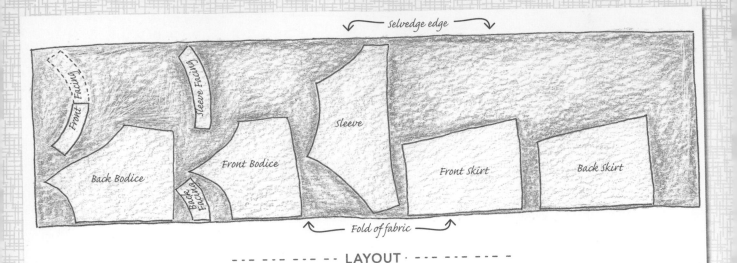

LAYOUT

From the tissue pattern, use the hip-length cutting line on the skirt portion of the pattern. Cut all pattern pieces from the main fabric. The layout above shows how to place the pieces if you're using fabric with a directional print. If there is no apparent direction to the print, then lay the pieces out however best conserves fabric, making sure to follow the grainline. **Special Cutting Note:** For sizes XL and XXL, the fabric will need to be opened out in order to accommodate the sleeve width. *This differs from the pictorial representation of the layout.*

CONSTRUCTION

Complete the steps in **General Construction** from *Prepare the Facings* through *Add the Sleeves and Facings.*

CONTRASTING HEM BAND

1. Begin by trying on the tunic and deciding on the finished length. Attaching the contrasting hem band will add approximately 2" to the finished design. You can shorten the tunic by simply trimming off an even amount all the way around the bottom edge.

2. For the hem band, cut two 5"-wide strips from the contrast fabric by the width of the fabric. Piece these strips, right sides together, with a ¼" seam allowance along one of the narrow ends to form one long strip. Press the seam open. (figure 1)

3. Fold the strip in half lengthwise, wrong sides together, with raw edges even and press. Open out the strip and press in ½" toward the wrong side along one narrow end, then fold in half again.

choosing fabric

When choosing fabric for this design, study the main fabric choice carefully. If the design only goes one way, it is considered to have fabric directionality and you will need to lay out all pieces in the same direction in order to maintain the integrity of the design. If the fabric has no apparent directionality, then the pieces may be laid out in either direction, as to conserve fabric.

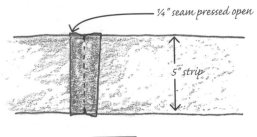

FIGURE 1

4. Place the pressed end of the strip against the right side of the tunic at one of the side seams, with raw edges even. Begin stitching approximately 2" in from the side seam and stitch all the way around until the beginning, stopping 2" before the side seam. (figure 2)

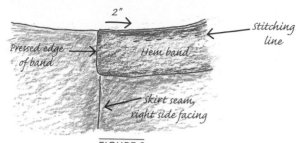

FIGURE 2

5. Lap the band over the portion that has been sewn, so 1" extends past the pressed end. Trim away any remaining portion. (figure 3)

6. Open the pressed end of the band and place the cut end inside. Keeping all raw edges together, finish stitching the seam. (figures 4a, 4b)

7. Press the seam toward the skirt portion of the tunic. Beginning at the side seam, edgestitch the band close to the tunic skirt seam. Topstitch ¼" away from the previous row of stitching. Pivot at the side seam and stitch to the bottom edge. Edgestitch along the bottom. (figure 5)

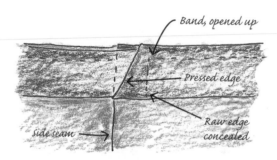

FIGURE 3

TIE BELT

1. For the tie belt, cut 2½"-wide by the width of the fabric strips as follows, according to size:

   XXS, XS, S: 2 strips

   M, L, XL, XXL: 3 strips

2. Piece the strips, right sides together, along the narrow ends with a ¼" seam allowance. Press the seams open.

3. Fold the strip in half lengthwise, right sides together, and stitch along the long raw edge with a ¼" seam allowance, forming a tube. Use a large safety pin or turning device to turn the tube right-side out and press, with the seam along one side.

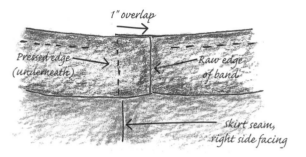

FIGURE 4A

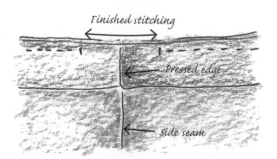

FIGURE 4B

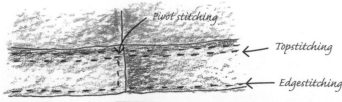

FIGURE 5

Back Bodice

Top edge of belt aligned with seam

Skirt Back

FIGURE 6

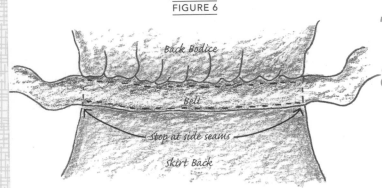

Back Bodice

Belt

Stop at side seams

Skirt Back

FIGURE 7

End of belt

Turn ¼" to inside

FIGURE 8

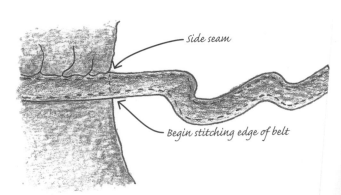

Side seam

Begin stitching edge of belt

FIGURE 9

4. Center the tube tie along the Back Bodice and Back Skirt seam. Pin in place with the top edge of the belt along the seam, stopping at the side seams. (figure 6)

5. Edgestitch both sides of the belt in place, stopping at the side seams. (figure 7)

6. Try on the tunic. Bring the tie belt around to the front, cross the ends, and wrap around to the back once more and tie in a knot. Trim away excess length equally from both tie ends. You should have enough to tie the belt and have it hang nearly to the bottom hem.

7. On each cut end of the belt, turn in approximately ¼" to the inside and press. (figure 8)

8. Finish the belt ends by edgestitching the remainder, starting where the belt joins at the side seams, across the end, and up the other side. Repeat for both sides. (figure 9)

make it your own

In making this design your own, you can opt to wear it plain without a belt, or make the belt from the same fabric as the tunic itself and hem it without a contrast as noted in General Construction. Another idea would be to use a decorative ribbon as the belt. The choice of fabric makes the strongest statement here. If you want something classic and subtle, choose a more subdued print. If you want to make a real statement, choose fabrics with high contrast values, such as black and white, red and white, or geometric patterns.

Materials list

Main Fabric (skirt portion):
  All Sizes: 1 yard
Contrast Fabric A (bodice
  and sleeves):
  Sizes XXS–L: 1½ yards
  Sizes XL & XXL: 2 yards
Contrast Fabric B (ruffle,
  sleeve band and tie belt):
  All Sizes: ¾ yard
*Yardages for all fabrics based on
  45"-wide cotton fabric*

Other Supplies

¼ yard of 20"-wide fusible
  interfacing for light- to
  medium-weight fabrics
14" invisible zipper
Polyester machine thread to
  match fabrics
Rotary cutter, ruler and mat
  (optional)
½ yard of ⅜"-wide elastic
Ruffler attachment for
  sewing machine (optional,
  but very convenient)
Scissors
Chalk pencil

RUFFLE-TRIMMED TUNIC

THE RUFFLE-TRIMMED TUNIC is a great way to use three coordinating fabrics in a creative way. This hip-length tunic features the boldest print on the skirt portion, where it can be shown without the interruption of a lot of seams or gathering. The other two prints are used as accents. I used the striped fabric for the tie belt, sleeve trim, and ruffle at the hem. I love using stripes this way; they seem to take on another texture and personality when gathered. I recommend including some sort of stripe when choosing fabrics for this design.

MY INITIAL SKETCH

When it came to the fabric, I knew I wanted a botanical feel. The large-scale print on the final tunic brought in that element, and coordinates from the same line add some fun.

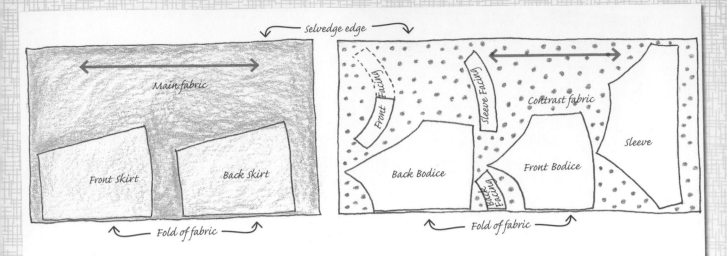

- - - - - - LAYOUT - - - - - - -

From the tissue pattern, use the hip-length cutting line on the skirt portion of the pattern. Cut the Front and Back Skirt pieces from the main fabric and all other pattern pieces from contrast fabric A. (Also cut the Front and Back Facings from interfacing.) The layout above shows how to place the pieces if you're using fabric with a directional print. If there is no apparent direction to the print, then lay the pieces out however best conserves fabric, making sure to follow the grainline. **Special Cutting Note:** For sizes XL and XXL, fabric will need to be opened out in order to accommodate the sleeve width. *This differs from the pictorial representation of the layout.*

- - - - - - CONSTRUCTION - - - - - - -

Complete the steps in **General Construction** for *Prepare the Facings*, then follow the instructions here, referring back to the **General Construction** as indicated.

Skirt, right side
(same for Front and
Back skirt)

FIGURE 1

PREPARE AND ATTACH THE RUFFLE AND BACK TIE

1. Cut two 3"-wide strips by the width of the fabric from contrast fabric B.

2. Fold each strip lengthwise, wrong sides together, with raw edges even, and press.

3. Use a long, straight stitch to sew two rows, one at ¼" and one at ⅜" from the raw edges. Create gathers by pulling on the bobbin threads. Or use a ruffler attachment to gather at every 6th stitch, sewing along the length of the raw edges approximately ⅜" from the edge. Press flat.

4. Pin the ruffle, right sides together, to the top edge of the Back Skirt piece, leaving approximately 1" extra at each side. Stitch with a ⅜" seam allowance. Repeat for the Front Skirt piece. (figure 1)

5. For the back tie belt, cut two 2½"-wide by the width of the fabric strips from contrast fabric B.

6. Fold each strip in half lengthwise, right sides together, and with raw edges even. Stitch down the long sides with a ¼" seam allowance, forming a tube. Turn right side out and press with the seam along one edge.

7. Edgestitch down both long edges of strips.

8. Pin the ties 3" down from the top raw edge of the Back Skirt piece, keeping raw edges even. (figure 2)

9. Stitch across the end, ⅜" in from the edge. The open ends will be finished in a later step, once the tunic has been tried on and the desired length is determined.

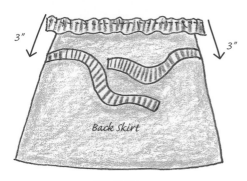

FIGURE 2

FIGURE 3

ATTACHING THE BODICE AND SKIRT PIECES

1. Complete the steps in **General Construction** for *Prepare the Facings* and *Attach the Bodice and Skirt Pieces* through step 5.

2. Press the seam toward the skirt with the ruffle turned up toward the bodice. Trim away the excess ruffle that extends beyond the raw edges on either side. (figure 3)

3. Continue with the steps in **General Construction**, picking up at step 6 in *Attach the Bodice and Skirt Pieces*. Complete the rest of the instructions through *Add the Sleeves and Facings*, remembering to cut the sleeve band from the contrast fabric B.

CONTRASTING RUFFLE HEM

1. Cut a series of strips for the ruffle hem from contrast fabric B: for sizes XXS–S, cut two 4"-wide by the width of the fabric strips; and for sizes M–XXL, cut three 4"-wide by the width of the fabric strips. Piece the strips, right sides together, along the narrow edges to form one long strip using a ¼" seam allowance. Press the seams open.

2. Fold the strip in half lengthwise, wrong sides together, with raw edges even and press.

3. Use a long, straight stitch to sew two rows from the raw edges, one at ¼" and one at ⅜". Create gathers by pulling on the bobbin threads. Or use a ruffler attachment to gather at every 6th stitch, sewing along the length of the raw edges approximately ⅜" from the edge. Press flat.

4. Beginning at one of the side seams, pin the ruffle to the right side of the skirt piece with raw edges even. Overlap the ends 2" beyond the seamline in each direction. (figure 4)

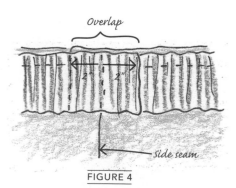

FIGURE 4

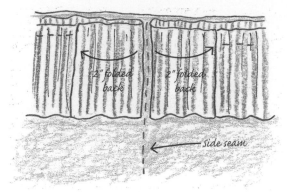

FIGURE 5

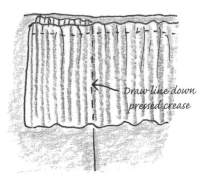

FIGURE 6

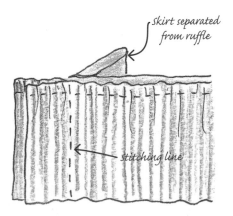

FIGURE 7

5. Begin stitching the ruffle in place, starting 2" in from the side seam using a ½" seam allowance. Stitch all the way around, stopping 2" before the side seam. Clip the threads.

6. Fold back both ends of the ruffle on itself, even with the side seam, and press. (figure 5) Draw a line in the creases of the ruffle just pressed. (figure 6)

7. Trim the ruffle ends to within 1" of the markings. With right sides together, match the markings and stitch the ruffle ends together. (figure 7)

8. Stitch again in the seam allowance to reinforce the seam, approximately ⅛" away from the original stitching. Trim the seam down, and press to one side.

9. Pin the open area of the ruffle to the skirt, matching the ruffle seam to the side seam and complete the stitching.

10. Serge or trim and finish the seam edge with a zigzag stitch. Press the seam toward the skirt.

11. Double topstitch the skirt close to the seamline.

FINISH THE TIE BELT

1. To finish the tie belt, try the tunic on and tie the belt in a knot or bow at the back waistline. Determine the desired length of the ties and trim an equal amount from each tie end.

2. On each tie end, turn in the raw edges ¼" twice to conceal the ends and press. Edgestitch across each end.

make it your own

In making this design your own, you can opt to wear it with or without the tie belt, or only place the waistline ruffle on the front. You can also opt to make the bodice and sleeve portion out of the same fabric as the skirt and use a contrast only for the sleeve bands, belt and ruffles. To determine yardage for this look, add the amounts for the main fabric and contrast fabric A together. You will still need the same amount for contrast fabric B.

Materials list

Main Fabric:

Sizes XXS - L: 2½ yards

Sizes XL - XXL: 2¾ yards

Contrast Fabric—For all
sizes, based on 45"-wide
fabric (frayed strips for
sleeve bands, waist, ruffle
hem and flower): ½ yard

Other Supplies

¼ yard of 20"-wide fusible
interfacing for light- to
medium-weight fabrics

14" invisible zipper

Polyester machine thread to
match fabrics

Rotary cutter, ruler and mat
(optional)

Scissors

½ yard of ⅜"-wide elastic

Ruffler attachment for
sewing machine (optional,
but very convenient)

Chalk pencil

Hand-sewing needle

THE FRAYED TUNIC DRESS portrays a touch of shabby elegance with the addition of frayed strips of fabric at the sleeve line, waist and hem. I chose a large-scale floral and coordinated with a soft pastel color palette so that the frayed edges would be prominent. A bold fabric can be chosen here, but the design elements might get lost in the busyness of the print.

MY INITIAL SKETCH

I was leaning toward large-scale pastel florals for this dress. When I found this lovely fabric in its cool shades of aqua and gray, I knew it was ideal. Adding the frayed flower at the neckline was the perfect accent for pulling the coordinates together.

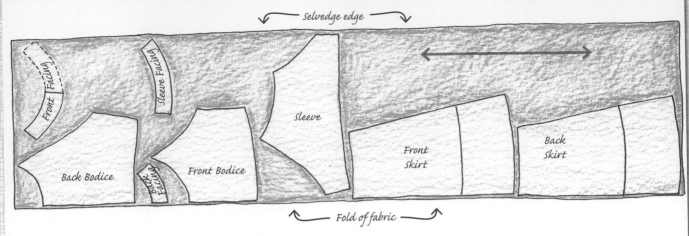

Front Facing

Sleeve Facing

Sleeve

Front
Skirt

Back
Skirt

Back Bodice

Back Facing

Front Bodice

Fold of fabric

LAYOUT

Use the above knee-length cutting line on the skirt portion of the pattern. Cut all pieces from the main fabric. (Also cut the Front and Back Facings from interfacing.) Note that the layout is shown with all pieces going the same way for fabric with a directional pattern. If there is no apparent direction to the print, then pieces can be laid out in either direction to conserve fabric, making sure to follow the grainline. **Special Cutting Note:** For sizes XL & XXL, fabric will need to be opened out in order to accommodate the sleeve width. *This differs from the pictorial representation of the layout.*

CONSTRUCTION

Complete the steps in **General Construction** for *Prepare the Facings*, then follow the instructions here, referring back to the **General Construction** as indicated.

PREPARE AND ATTACH THE RAW EDGE RUFFLES

1. Cut two 1½"-wide strips by the width of the fabric from contrast fabric.

2. Use a long, straight stitch to sew two rows, one at ¼" and one at ⅜" from the raw edges. Create gathers by pulling on the bobbin threads. Or use a ruffler attachment to gather at every 6th stitch, sewing along the length of the raw edges approximately ⅜" from the edge. (See page 27.) Press flat.

3. Pin the ruffle to the top edge of the Front Skirt piece, right sides together, leaving approximately ½" extra at each side, and stitch with a ⅜" seam allowance. Repeat for the Back Skirt piece. (figure 1)

ATTACH THE BODICE AND SKIRT PIECES

1. Complete the steps in **General Construction** for *Prepare the Facings* and *Attach the Bodice and Skirt Pieces* through step 3.

2. With wrong sides together, match the center mark of each bodice piece with a skirt piece and pin in place. Pin side edges in place and then gently pull the bobbin threads to gather the bodice until it matches in size with the top of each skirt piece. Distribute the gathers evenly and stitch together, using a ½" seam allowance.

½"   ½"

Ruffle, right side

skirt, right side
(same for Front
and Back Skirt)

FIGURE 1

3. Press the exposed seam down toward the skirt. Topstitch in place by stitching over the lowest gathering stitch. Trim the excess ruffle strip even with the side edges of the skirt. (figure 2)

4. Press intentional creases in the Front and Back Bodice pieces to make the gathering lie flat (see page 21). Continue with the steps in **General Construction**, beginning with step 7 in *Attach the Bodice and Skirt Pieces*. Complete the rest of the instructions through *Sew the Side Seam and Sleeves* (step 8). Note in step 6, cut the sleeve band 3"-wide by your arm measurement from the main fabric.

5. Use either the remaining ruffle piece or cut another 1½"-wide strip and gather it as before. Press the strip flat.

6. Match the gathered edge of the ruffle strip against the raw edges of the band. With ½" of the ruffle extending beyond the band seamline, stitch the ruffle to the band, ⅜" from the raw edges and overlap the ruffle by ½" to finish. Cut away excess ruffle. Repeat for the other arm band. (figure 3)

7. Pin the band to the sleeve, wrong sides together. Match the center snips and seams. Pull the gathering threads along the edge of the sleeve until it matches the band in size. Evenly distribute the gathers and stitch in place using a ½" seam allowance. (figure 4)

8. Press the sleeve seam toward the band and topstitch over the outer line of gathering stitches.

9. Complete the steps in **General Construction** for *Add the Sleeves and Facings*.

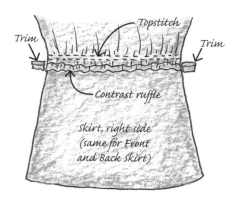

FIGURE 2

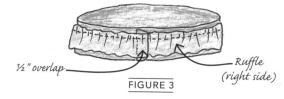

FIGURE 3

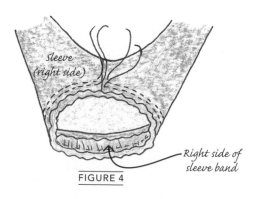

FIGURE 4

- - - - - - ADD THE RUFFLE HEM - - - - - -

1. Cut a series of 3"-wide by the width of the fabric strips from the contrast fabric for the ruffle hem. For sizes XXS–S, cut two strips. For M–XXL, cut three strips. Piece the strips, right sides together, with a ¼" seam allowance along the ends to form one long strip. Clean-finish the seam and press to one side.

2. Use a long, straight stitch to sew two rows, one at ¼" and one at ⅜" from the raw edges. Create gathers by pulling on the bobbin threads. Or use a ruffler attachment to gather at every 6th stitch, sewing along the length of the raw edges approximately ⅜" from the edge. Press flat.

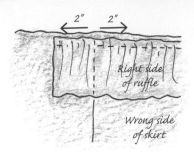

FIGURE 5

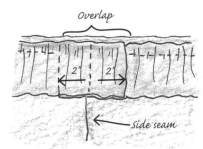

FIGURE 6

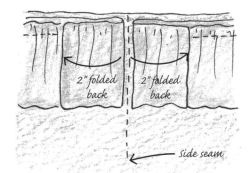

FIGURE 7A

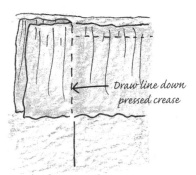

FIGURE 7B

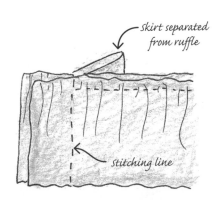

FIGURE 8

3. Beginning at one of the side seams, pin the ruffle to the skirt piece, wrong sides together with raw edges even. Overlap the ends 2" beyond the seamline in each direction. (figure 5)

4. Begin stitching the ruffle in place, starting 2" away from the side seam using a ½" seam allowance. Stitch all the way around, stopping 2" before the beginning. Clip the threads. (figure 6)

5. Fold back both ends of the ruffle on itself even with the side seam and press. (figure 7a) Draw a line in the creases of the ruffle just pressed. (figure 7b)

6. Trim the ruffle ends to within 1" of the markings. With right sides together, match up the markings and stitch the ruffle ends together. (figure 8)

7. Stitch again in the seam allowance to reinforce the seam, approximately ⅛" away from the original stitching. Press the seam to one side.

8. Pin the open area of the ruffle to the skirt, matching the ruffle seam to the side, and complete the stitching.

9. Open the ruffle away from the skirt and press the seam upward toward the skirt.

10. Topstitch the ruffle by stitching over the top line of the gathering stitches.

- - - - CREATE AND ADD FLOWER - - - -

1. To make the flower, cut one 2"-wide by the width of the fabric strip from the contrast fabric.

2. Fold in half lengthwise, wrong sides together, with raw edges even, and press.

3. Use a long, straight stitch to sew two rows, one at ¼" and one at ⅜" from the raw edges. Create gathers by pulling on the bobbin threads. Or use a ruffler attachment to gather at every 6th stitch, sewing along the length of the raw edges approximately ¼" from the edge.

4. Thread a hand-sewing needle with matching thread and knot. Beginning at one end of the strip, fold down the corner diagonally toward the raw gathered edge.

5. Secure with needle and thread, then trim off the corner. (figure 9) Continue rolling up the strip, taking stitches along raw edges as needed to secure the layers. Use as much of the strip as you like to make the desired size. If you want a smaller flower, just cut away any excess.

6. Finish by turning in the remaining end diagonally toward the inside of the flower and stitch in place. Trim off the remaining corner. (figure 10)

7. Stitch or pin the flower in place at the left neckline of the dress.

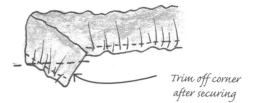

Trim off corner after securing

FIGURE 9

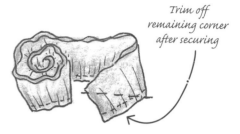

Trim off remaining corner after securing

FIGURE 10

make it your own

In making this design your own, you could make the top portion from a contrast fabric and add a third fabric for the frayed ruffles. Follow the yardage requirements for the Ruffle-Trimmed Tunic for the bodice and sleeves and increase the yardage for the skirt to include the longer length, approximately 1½ yards. You could also make more flowers and add one to the lower edge where the skirt and ruffle trim meet.

GEOMETRIC TUNIC DRESS

Materials list

Main Fabric (bodice, sleeves, and upper skirt):

Sizes XXS–L: 2¼ yards

Sizes XL & XXL: 2¾ yards

Contrast Fabric (lower skirt, sleeve bands, and waist trim):

All Sizes: ¾ yard

Yardages for all fabrics based on 45"-wide cotton fabric

Other Supplies

¼ yard of 20"-wide fusible interfacing for light- to mid-weight fabrics

½ yard of ⅜"-wide elastic

14" invisible zipper

Polyester machine thread to match

Rotary Cutter, ruler and mat (optional)

Scissors

Chalk pencil

THE GEOMETRIC TUNIC DRESS is fun and funky with bold prints in geometric patterns and swirls. This is definitely the "mod" variation, so be uninhibited with your fabric choices. Go for large-scale prints in bright colors, or all black and white. This above-the-knee-length stunner is sure to get attention every time you wear it!

MY INITIAL SKETCH

I originally envisioned this design in bright primary colors, but then I found this vibrant green print. When I paired it with the graphic black-and-white fabric, I knew I had a winning combination!

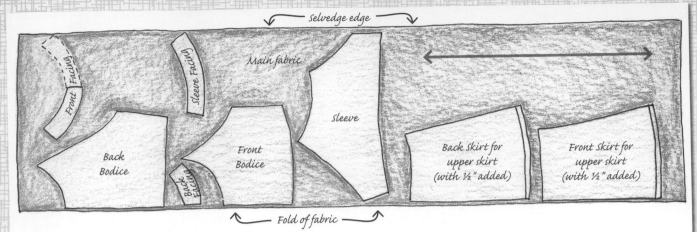

selvedge edge

Front Facing

Sleeve Facing

Main fabric

sleeve

Back Bodice

Back Facing

Front Bodice

Back Skirt for upper skirt (with ½" added)

Front Skirt for upper skirt (with ½" added)

Fold of fabric

LAYOUT

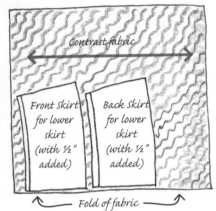

Contrast fabric

Front Skirt for lower skirt (with ½" added)

Back Skirt for lower skirt (with ½" added)

Fold of fabric

From the pattern, use the hip-length cutting line on the Front and Back Skirt for the upper skirt; add a ½" seam allowance to the lower edge. Use the Front and Back Skirt pattern piece from below the hip-length line to the above-knee-length line for the lower skirt, adding a ½" seam allowance to the top edge. Cut all pieces from the fabrics as indicated. (Also cut the Front and Back Facings from interfacing.) The layout shows how to place the pieces if you're using fabric with a directional print. If there is no apparent direction to the print, then lay the pieces out however best conserves fabric, making sure to follow the grainline. **Special Cutting Note:** For sizes XL & XXL, the fabric will need to be opened out in order to accommodate the sleeve width. *This differs from the pictorial representation of the layout.*

CONSTRUCTION

Complete the steps in **General Construction** for *Prepare the Facings*, then follow the instructions here, referring back to the **General Construction** as indicated.

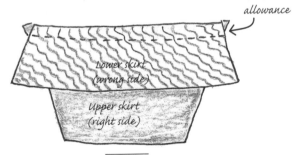

½" seam allowance

Lower skirt (wrong side)

Upper skirt (right side)

FIGURE 1

SEWING SKIRT SECTIONS TOGETHER

1. Pin the upper and lower sections of the skirt, right sides together, matching the raw edges. Stitch the two sections together with a ½" seam allowance and press the seam toward the upper skirt. Repeat for the remaining skirt pieces. (figure 1)

2. Edgestitch on the main fabric next to the seam, then complete another two rows of stitching approximately ¼" away from each other for a total of three lines of stitching. (figure 2)

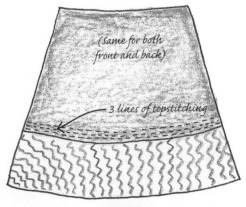

(same for both front and back)

3 lines of topstitching

FIGURE 2

PREPARE AND ATTACH CONTRAST BAND AT WAISTLINE

1. Cut two 3"-wide by the width of the fabric strips from the contrast fabric. Fold each in half lengthwise, wrong sides together, with the raw edges even, and press.

2. Pin a strip, right sides together, to the top edge of each skirt piece leaving approximately ½" extending at each side. Stitch with a ⅜" seam allowance. (figure 3)

3. Trim any excess strip from the sides. (figure 4)

4. Complete the steps in **General Construction**, under *Attach the Bodice and Skirt Pieces* through step 5. (You'll skip steps 6 and 7). Press the contrast strip up toward the bodice. Edgestitch next to the seamline and then complete two more rows of stitching ¼" away as was done on the skirt pieces. (figure 4)

5. Continue again with the steps in **General Construction** starting at *Install the Zipper* and complete all the steps through *Add the Hem*. Remember to cut the sleeve band from the contrast fabric.

ADD DECORATIVE TOPSTITCHING AND HEM

1. Add a third row of decorative topstitching at the neckline, placing it between the two existing rows of stitching.

2. At the hem edge, add two more rows of topstitching ¼" away from each other to form three rows of stitching as was done on the neckline and at the Contrasting Band.

3. Edgestitch along the pressed edge at the bottom of the hem.

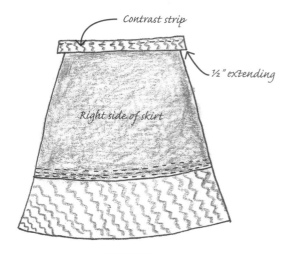

Contrast strip

½" extending

Right side of skirt

FIGURE 3

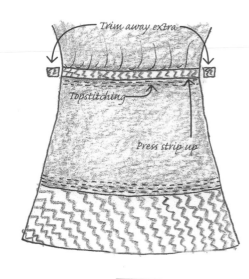

Trim away extra

Topstitching

Press strip up

FIGURE 4

make it your own

In making this design your own, you could make it into a tunic-length version by using the hip-length line on the skirt pattern and then adding a contrast band as was completed for the Damask Tunic. Follow the fabric requirements as outlined for that particular variation. You could also go the opposite way and make the dress a longer length by cutting along the above-knee-length line for the upper skirt and using the very bottom portion for the contrast. Don't forget to add a ½" seam allowance to the pieces so that no length is lost in the process of sewing. Also remember that this will probably add about a ½ yard to the overall fabric requirements for the main fabric.

FLIRTY TUNIC DRESS

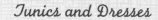

Materials list

Main Fabric (bodice, sleeves, and upper skirt):

Sizes XXS–L: 2¾ yards

Sizes XL & XXL: 3 yards

Contrast Fabric (lower skirt, sleeve band and waist trim):

All Sizes: 1 yard

Yardages for all fabrics based on 45"-wide cotton fabric

Other Supplies

¼ yard of 20"-wide fusible interfacing for light- to medium-weight fabrics:

½ yard of ⅜" wide elastic

14" invisible zipper

Polyester machine thread to match fabrics

Rotary Cutter, ruler and mat (optional)

Scissors

Chalk pencil

THE FLIRTY TUNIC DRESS has feminine detailing with a large contrast ruffle and a tie belt that crosses in the back. This below-the-knee-length design works well for fabrics with large motifs of birds or flowers in soft vibrant colors. Choose two coordinates with high contrast so that the details stand out nicely and contribute to the overall style of this dress variation.

MY INITIAL SKETCH

In this sketch, I paired vivid pinks and greens, and was able to remain true to my sketch. I love the chandelier and birds motif in this fabric. This dress looks lovely with the Cozy Wool Jacket (page 134).

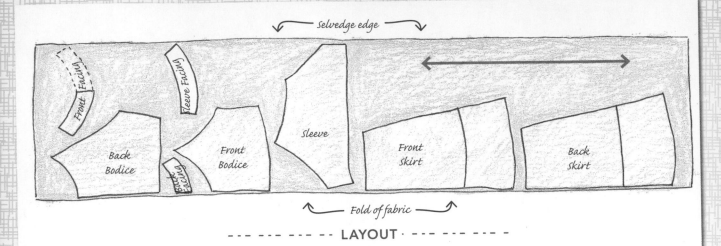

Selvedge edge

Front Facing

Sleeve Facing

Back Bodice

Back Facing

Front Bodice

Sleeve

Front Skirt

Back Skirt

Fold of fabric

LAYOUT

From the pattern, use the above-knee-length cutting line for the skirt portion. Cut all pieces from the main fabric. (Also cut the Front and Back Facings from interfacing.) The layout shows how to place the pieces if you're using fabric with a directional print. If there is no apparent direction to the print, then lay the pieces out however best conserves fabric making sure to follow the grainline. **Special Cutting Note:** For sizes XL & XXL, fabric will need to be opened out in order to accommodate the sleeve width. This differs from the pictorial representation of the layout.

CONSTRUCTION

Complete the steps in **General Construction** from *Prepare the Facings* through *Add the Sleeves and Facings*, cutting the sleeve band from the main fabric.

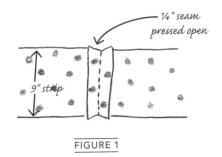

¼" seam pressed open

9" strip

FIGURE 1

RUFFLE HEM

1. Cut two strips from the contrast fabric, 9"-wide by the width of the fabric. Sew the two strips together with a ¼" seam allowance at the narrow ends to form one long strip. Press the seam open. (figure 1)

2. Use a long, straight stitch to sew two rows, one at ¼" and one at ⅜" from the raw edges. Create gathers by pulling on the bobbin threads. Or use a ruffler attachment to gather at every 6th stitch, sewing along the length of the raw edges approximately ⅜" from the edge. (See page 27.) Press flat.

3. Beginning at one of the side seams, pin the ruffle to the skirt piece, right sides together, with raw edges even. Overlap the ends 2" beyond the seamline in each direction. Begin stitching the ruffle in place, starting 2" in from the side seam using a ½" seam allowance. (figures 2 and 3)

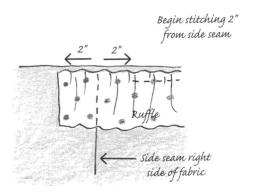

Begin stitching 2" from side seam

2" 2"

Ruffle

side seam right side of fabric

FIGURE 2

4. Stitch all the way around, stopping 2" before the side seam. Clip the threads. (figure 3)

5. Fold back both ends of the ruffle on itself even with the side seam and press. (figure 4) Draw a line in the creases of the ruffle just pressed. (figure 5)

6. Trim the ruffle ends to within 1" of the markings. With right sides together, match the markings and stitch the ruffle ends together. (figure 6)

7. Stitch again in the seam allowance to reinforce the seam, approximately ⅛" away from the original stitching. Trim the seam down and press to one side.

8. Pin the open area of the ruffle to the skirt, matching the ruffle seam to the side seam, and complete the stitching. (figure 7)

9. Open the ruffle away from the skirt and press the seam upward toward the skirt.

10. Serge or trim and finish the seam with a zigzag stitch.

11. Edgestitch the lower edge of the skirt next to the seamline, then stitch again ¼" away from stitching.

12. Finish the bottom edge of the ruffle with a zigzag stitch or serge. Press up 1" of the ruffle to the wrong side to form the hem. Stitch on the right side, ¾" from the pressed edge, then again ¼" below. Press the ruffle flat.

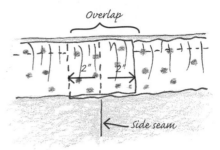

FIGURE 3

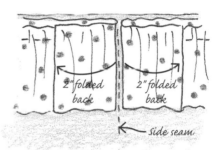

FIGURE 4

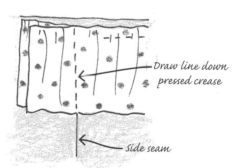

FIGURE 5

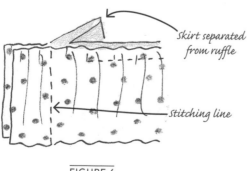

FIGURE 6

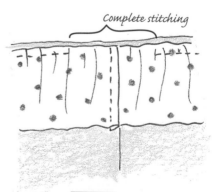

FIGURE 7

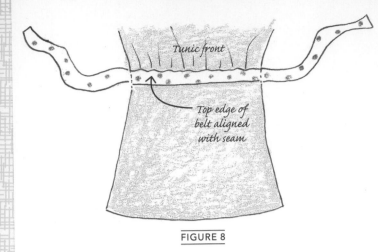

Tunic front

Top edge of
belt aligned
with seam

FIGURE 8

1. For the tie belt, cut 2½"-wide strips by the width of the fabric as follows: for sizes XXS–S, cut two strips; for sizes M–XXL, cut three strips

2. Piece the strips, right sides together, at the narrow end with a ¼" seam allowance. Press the seams open.

3. Fold the strip in half lengthwise, right sides together, and stitch along the length of the raw edge with a ¼" seam allowance, forming a tube. Use a large safety pin or turning device to turn the tube right side out. Press with the seam along one side.

4. Center the belt along the Front Bodice and Front Skirt seam. Pin in place with the top edge of the belt along the seam, stopping at the side seams. (figure 8)

5. Edgestitch the top and bottom edges of the belt on the Front Skirt, stopping at the side seams. (figure 9)

6. Try on the tunic. Bring the tie belt around to the back, cross the ends, and wrap around to the front once more and tie in a bow. Trim away any excess length equally from both ends. You should have enough to tie the belt and have it hang nearly to the bottom hem.

7. On each cut end of the tie belt, turn in approximately ¼" to the inside and press. (figure 10)

8. Finish the belt and ends by edgestitching starting where the belt joins at the side seams, across the end, and up the other side. (figure 11)

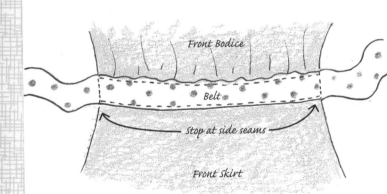

Front Bodice

Belt

Stop at side seams

Front Skirt

FIGURE 9

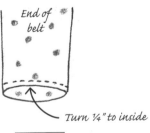

End of belt

Turn ¼" to inside

FIGURE 10

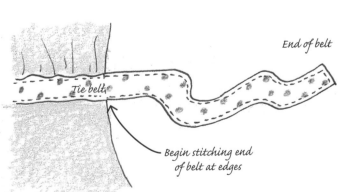

End of belt

Tie belt

Begin stitching end of belt at edges

FIGURE 11

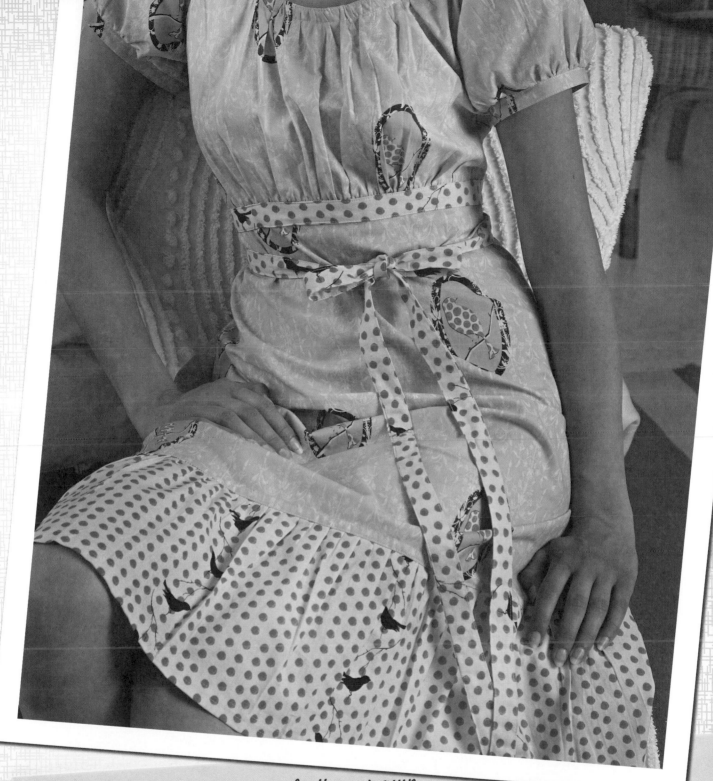

make it your own

In making this design your own, you can opt to wear it plain without a belt, or make the belt from the same fabric as the tunic itself and hem it without a contrast as noted in General Construction. Another idea would be to use a decorative ribbon as the belt. The choice of fabric makes the strongest statement here. If you want something classic and subtle, choose a more subdued print. If you want to make a real statement, choose fabrics with high contrast values, such as black and white, red and white, or geometric patterns.

ROMANTIC FLORAL TUNIC DRESS

Materials list

Main Fabric (bodice, sleeves,
and skirt):
All Sizes: 3¼ yards
Contrast Fabric (ruffle, sleeve
band and waist trim):
All Sizes: ½ yard
*Yardages for all fabrics based on
45"-wide cotton fabric*

Other Supplies

¼ yard of 20"-wide fusible
interfacing for light- to
mid-weight fabrics
½ yard of ⅜"-wide elastic
14" invisible zipper
Polyester machine thread to
match fabrics
Rotary cutter, ruler and mat
(optional)
Scissors
Chalk pencil

THE ROMANTIC FLORAL TUNIC DRESS is perfect for a large-scale floral fabric. The design pictured features a border print fabric. Because the border print follows the length rather than width of the fabric, the fabric was opened out and folded in the opposite manner than how it came on the bolt to fully utilize the fading effect of the design in the lines of the dress from neck to hem. If you choose a fabric that is not a border print, follow the cutting layout for the Flirty Tunic Dress, but use the longest length on the pattern pieces for the skirt.

MY INITIAL SKETCH

I originally planned to use a fabric with a large floral motif and little chandeliers. Because I used that fabric on the Flirty Tunic Dress (page 100), I went with a dramatic border print that fades so nicely from one pattern to another.

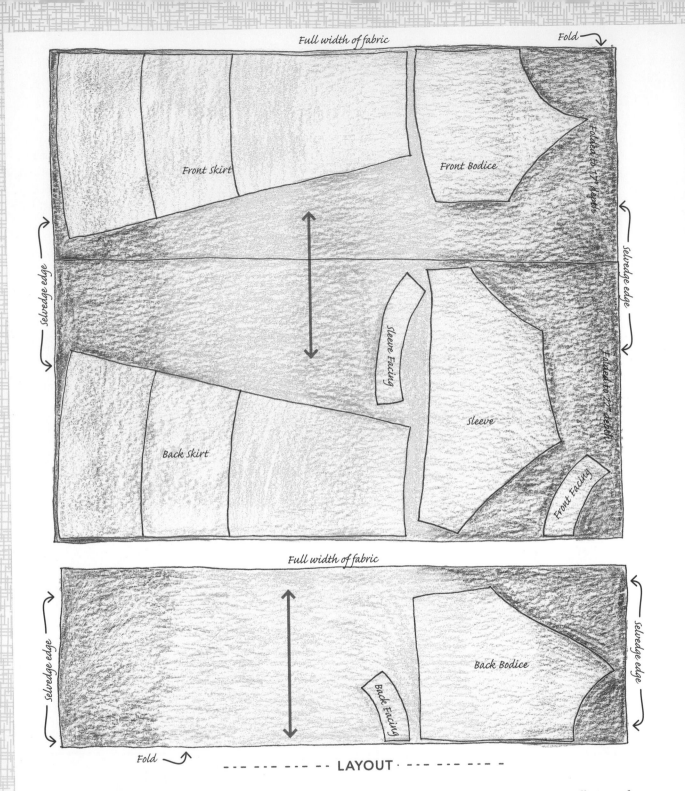

Full width of fabric

Fold

Front Skirt

Front Bodice

Folded to 17" depth

selvedge edge

selvedge edge

Sleeve Facing

Sleeve

Folded to 22" depth

Back Skirt

Front Facing

Full width of fabric

selvedge edge

Back Facing

Back Bodice

selvedge edge

Fold

· – – – · – – – · – – · · **LAYOUT** · – – · – – – · – – – · ·

From the pattern, use the below-knee-length cutting line on the Front and Back Skirt piece. Cut all pieces from the main fabric. (Also cut the Front and Back Facings from interfacing.) The layout shows how to place the pieces if you're using a border print fabric; note that the fabric is opened out, and then re-folded to take advantage of the width of the design. If you're using a fabric with a directional print, refer to the layout on page 102. If there is no apparent direction to the print, then lay the pieces out however best conserves fabric, making sure to follow the grainline.

· - - · - - - - CONSTRUCTION · - - - · - - - -

Complete the steps in **General Construction** from *Prepare the Facings* through *Add the Sleeves and Facings*, cutting the sleeve band from the contrast fabric.

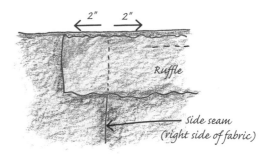

Ruffle

side seam
(right side of fabric)

FIGURE 1

· - - - · - - - ADD CONTRASTING RUFFLE HEM · - - - · - - -

1. Cut a series of strips from the contrast fabric B, 4"-wide by the width of the fabric for the ruffle hem. For sizes XXS–S, cut two strips; for M–XXL, cut three strips. Piece the strips, right sides together, along the narrow ends using a ¼" seam allowance to form one long strip. Press the seam open.

2. Fold the strip in half lengthwise, wrong sides together, with raw edges even, and press.

3. Use a long, straight stitch to sew two rows, one at ¼" and one at ⅜" from the raw edges. Create gathers by pulling on the bobbin threads. Or use a ruffler attachment to gather at every 6th stitch, sewing along the length of the raw edges approximately ⅜" from the edge. (See page 27.) Press flat.

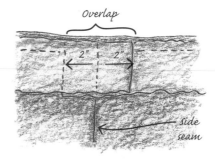

Overlap

side seam

FIGURE 2

4. Beginning at one of the side seams, pin the ruffle to the right side of the skirt with raw edges even. Overlap the ends 2" beyond the seamline in both directions. (figure 1)

5. Begin stitching the ruffle in place, starting 2" away from the side seam using a ½" seam allowance. Stitch all the way around, stopping 2" before the side seam. Clip the threads. (figure 2)

working with border prints

When working with a border print, it is important to be aware of how the pieces will fit together. In other words, make sure that the sleeves and bodice are from the same area of the fabric and that they are going in the same direction so that it will appear that the fabric is uninterrupted in flow once the dress is sewn together. Likewise, the skirt sections should be cut so that the basic motif of the fabric design is lined up along the hem and side seams.

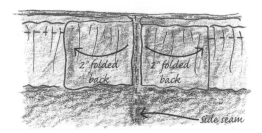

FIGURE 3

6. Fold back the ruffle on itself even with the side seam and press. Draw a line in the creases of the ruffle just pressed. (figures 3 and 4)

7. Trim the ruffle ends to within 1" of the markings. Match the markings and stitch the ruffle ends together. (figure 5)

8. Stitch again in the seam allowance to reinforce the seam, approximately ⅛" away from the original stitching. Trim the seam down and press to one side.

9. Pin the open area of the skirt, matching the ruffle seam to the side seam, and complete the stitching.

10. Serge or trim and clean-finish the seam edge with a zigzag stitch. Press the seam toward the skirt.

11. Double topstitch the skirt close to the seamline. (See page 21.)

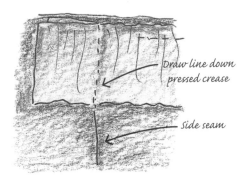

FIGURE 4

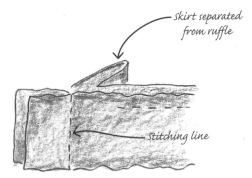

FIGURE 5

make it your own

To make this design your own, consider using two main fabrics that coordinate; one for the skirt and one for the bodice pieces. This will mean that you will need about 2 yards of the skirt fabric and 1½ yards for the bodice pieces. The contrast fabric for the sleeve bands and ruffle hem would stay the same. Of course a tie belt or flower from one of the other variations would look great on this design also. Have fun with the choices you make!

Chapter Three

JACKETS

JACKETS ARE SUCH A wonderful addition to a wardrobe! I love how they have a way of pulling an entire outfit together. Some jackets make a statement of their own with bold fabrics or special trims with lots of texture. The jackets in this section have their own star appeal as well as being just the perfect addition to an outfit. All six projects originate from one basic set of pattern pieces which features details such as a raglan three-quarter-length sleeve, raised waistline, and a semi-fitted A-line skirt with subtle gathering and featured in three lengths. Each project has its own individual detailing with the collar, cuffs, button tabs or a tie belt.

The following projects detail six variations: two at hip-length that can be worn with a skirt or pants, two fingertip-length and two knee-length jackets. Through the use of various fabric combinations and embellishments, each showcases its own unique style and yet remains simple to sew. Suggested fabrics for this design include linen, heavier weight cottons such as twills or velveteen, linen, and wool.

Once you have made muslins for this design following the recommendations in Custom Fitting, you will have a perfect-fitting jacket to show off a great piece of textured fabric!

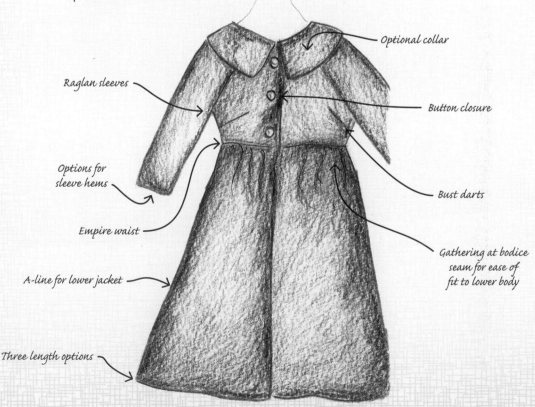

Optional collar

Raglan sleeves

Button closure

Options for sleeve hems

Bust darts

Empire waist

Gathering at bodice seam for ease of fit to lower body

A-line for lower jacket

Three length options

GENERAL CONSTRUCTION

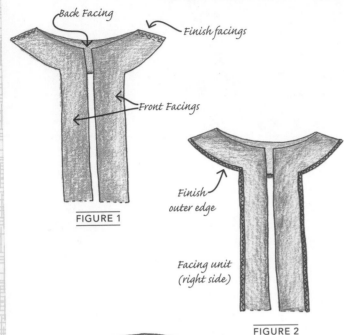

Back Facing
Finish facings
Front Facings

FIGURE 1

Finish outer edge

Facing unit (right side)

FIGURE 2

When cutting out the jacket pieces, be sure to clip all notches and mark the bodice darts as well as the center front at the neckline. Once the fabric pieces have been cut out and all markings have been transferred, remove the tissue pieces.

NOTE: All seam allowances are ½" unless otherwise stated.

PREPARE THE FACINGS

1. Apply fusible interfacing to the wrong side of the Front and Back Neck Facings, following the manufacturer's instructions.

2. Pin the Front Neck Facings to the Back Neck Facing, right sides together, at the shoulders and sew. Serge the seam allowances or trim and clean-finish with a zigzag stitch. (figure 1)

3. Press the seams to one side and clean-finish the lower edges of the facing unit with a serger or a zigzag stitch. (figure 2)

CREATE THE COLLAR

1. Apply fusible interfacing to the wrong side of one of the Collar pieces. Place Collar pieces right sides together, matching edges. Sew together along the outer curved edge and straight center front edges. (figure 3)

2. Trim the seam allowance to ¼" and clip the curve of the collar. Trim diagonally across the center front corners. (figure 4)

3. Turn the collar right side out, fully turning out the corners. Press, with the interfaced side facing up. This will be the side of the collar that will face up when the jacket is finished.

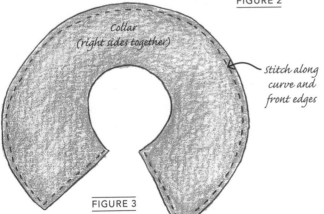

Collar (right sides together)

Stitch along curve and front edges

FIGURE 3

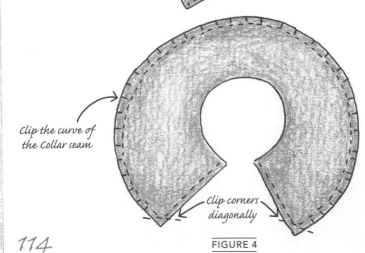

Clip the curve of the Collar seam

Clip corners diagonally

FIGURE 4

4. Edgestitch the edges of the collar and also baste the neckline closed, using a long stitch length, about ¼" in from the edges. (figure 5)

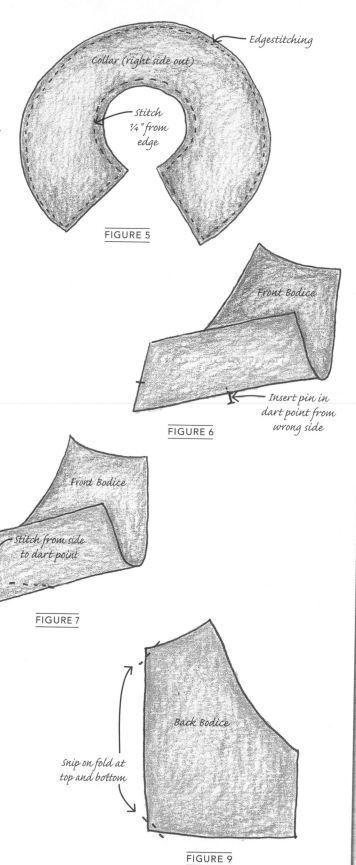

Collar (right side out)

Edgestitching

Stitch ¼" from edge

FIGURE 5

MAKE THE FRONT BODICE DARTS

1. To make the darts for the Front Bodice pieces, match the markings along the side seam of the bodice, right sides together. Insert a pin at the point of the dart. (figure 6)

2. Sew along the side markings and taper to the pin at the dart point. (figure 7)

3. Open the Front Bodice piece and press the dart down. After pressing, trim away any excess portion of the dart that extends beyond the side seam. Repeat these steps for the remaining Front Bodice piece. (figure 8)

Front Bodice

Insert pin in dart point from wrong side

FIGURE 6

SEW THE BODICE TOGETHER

1. Before unfolding the Back Bodice piece, snip the corners at the top and bottom, within the seam allowance to mark the center back. (figure 9)

Front Bodice

Stitch from side to dart point

FIGURE 7

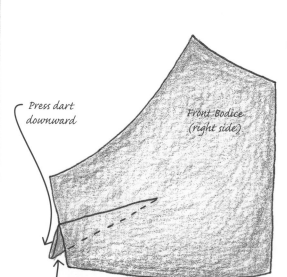

Press dart downward

Front Bodice (right side)

Trim away excess dart from side

FIGURE 8

Back Bodice

Snip on fold at top and bottom

FIGURE 9

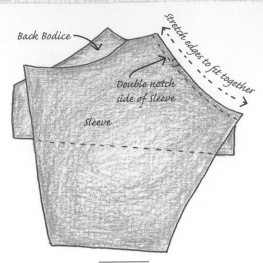

Back Bodice

Double notch side of Sleeve

Stretch edges to fit together

Sleeve

FIGURE 10

2. Match the two notches on the Sleeve piece with the notches on the Back Bodice piece, right sides together; pin. The top edges should be even with the lower edge of the Sleeve piece, slightly extending beyond the Back Bodice edge. Stretch the Sleeve pieces slightly during sewing to make the two pieces fit together. (figure 10)

3. Press the seam allowances toward the Back Bodice.

4. Pin each Front Bodice to the remaining sides of the Sleeve pieces with right sides together. The top edge of the Front Bodice will extend slightly beyond the Sleeve piece edge and the lower Sleeve piece edge will extend slightly beyond the Front Bodice. Stretch the pieces slightly during sewing to fit them together properly. (figure 11)

5. Press the seam allowances toward the Front Bodice.

6. Double topstitch (see page 21) the seams from the right side of the bodice. (figure 12)

7. Fold the sleeve in half lengthwise, right sides together, bringing the sleeve piece as well as the Front and Back Bodice side seams. Match the raw edges and pin. Make sure that the darts on the Front Bodice pieces are still pointing downward. Sew the sleeve and side seam. (figure 13)

8. Turn right side out and press the seams to one side.

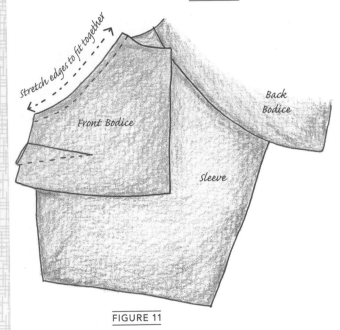

Stretch edges to fit together

Front Bodice

Back Bodice

Sleeve

FIGURE 11

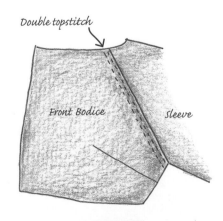

Double topstitch

Front Bodice

Sleeve

FIGURE 12

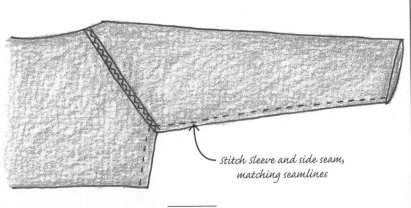

Stitch sleeve and side seam, matching seamlines

FIGURE 13

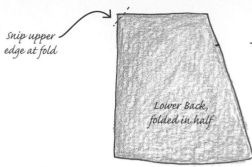

snip upper edge at fold

Lower Back, folded in half

FIGURE 14

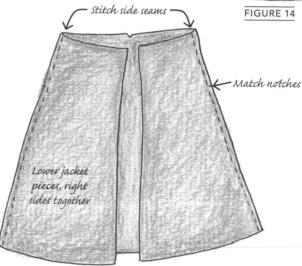

Stitch side seams

Match notches

Lower jacket pieces, right sides together

FIGURE 15

SEW THE LOWER JACKET TOGETHER

1. Before unfolding the Lower Back, snip the upper corner within the seam allowance. (figure 14)

2. Pin the Lower Front pieces to the Lower Back piece, right sides together, matching the raw edges and notches. Sew and press the seams to one side. (figure 15)

3. Use a long, straight stitch to sew two rows along the upper edge of the lower jacket, one at ¼" and one at ⅜". Begin and end the stitching approximately 2" from the side seams and front edges. (figure 16)

4. Pin the bodice and lower jacket pieces, right sides together, matching side seams and front edges, as well as center back markings. Gently pull gathering threads until the lower jacket matches the bodice in size. Distribute the gathers evenly and pin in place. (figure 17)

5. Stitch the bodice and lower jacket pieces together, using a ½" seam.

6. Trim the seam and serge or clean-finish the edges.

7. Press the seam toward the bodice. With the right side up, edgestitch along the bodice side of the seam. (figure 18)

8. Press intentional creases in the lower jacket to mimic pleating. (See page 21.)

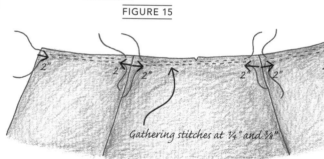

2" *2"* *2"* *2"* *2"*

Gathering stitches at ¼" and ⅜"

FIGURE 16

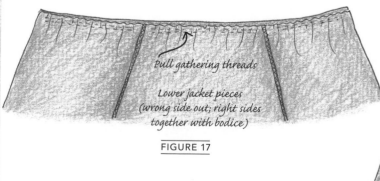

Pull gathering threads

Lower jacket pieces (wrong side out; right sides together with bodice)

FIGURE 17

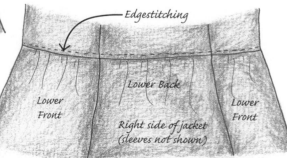

Edgestitching

Lower Front

Lower Back

Lower Front

Right side of jacket (sleeves not shown)

FIGURE 18

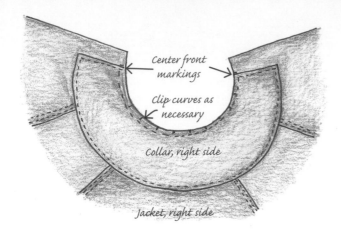

Center front markings

Clip curves as necessary

Collar, right side

Jacket, right side

FIGURE 19

ADD THE COLLAR

1. With the collar's top side up, pin the collar to the right side of the jacket neckline. The collar should start at one center front marking and end at the other. It may be necessary to clip the inner curve of the collar to make the pieces fit together smoothly. (figure 19)

2. Sew the collar to the jacket with a ½" seam, starting and stopping at the collar center front edges.

ADD THE FACINGS

1. Place the facing unit on the neckline and front edges of the jacket, right sides together, matching the raw edges. Pin in place. (figure 20)

2. Stitch the curve of the neckline first, following the previous line of stitching (if the collar was added).

3. Stitch down the center fronts, pivoting at the top center front corners. (figure 21)

4. Trim the seam allowance to ¼", cut diagonally across the top center front corners, and clip the neckline curve. (figure 22)

5. Understitch the seam allowance to the facing (see page 25).

6. Turn the facing to the inside of the jacket, turn out the corners and press. Pin the neck facing at the sleeve seams at the top of the jacket to hold them in place.

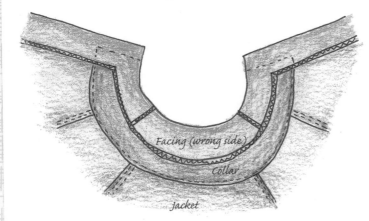

Facing (wrong side)

Collar

Jacket

FIGURE 20

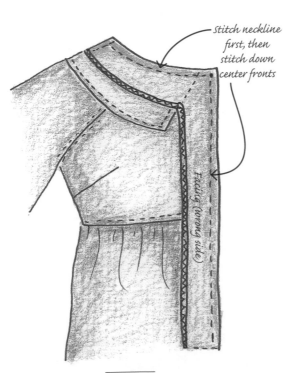

Stitch neckline first, then stitch down center fronts

Facing (wrong side)

FIGURE 21

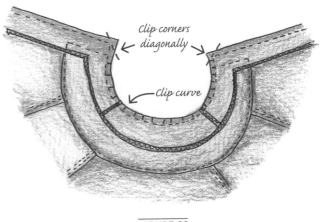

Clip corners diagonally

Clip curve

FIGURE 22

- - - - - - HEM THE BOTTOM - - - - - -

1. Fold the bottom of the facings back on the jacket, so that the right sides are together. Measure up 2" from the lower edge and mark across the facing. (figure 23)

2. Stitch across the facing through all thicknesses at the marking. Carefully trim away only the facing below the stitching line and trim away the corner diagonally through all thicknesses. (figure 24)

3. Serge or clean-finish the lower edge.

4. Turn the facing back to the inside of the jacket and fully turn out the corners and press.

5. Turn up the hem 2" to the inside of the jacket and press. You may experience slight pleating at the side seams. This is not a concern as they will be stitched in place when the hem is sewn. (figure 25)

6. Pin the facing in place along the center front edges of the jacket.

Fold facings back to outside of jacket along lower edge

FIGURE 23

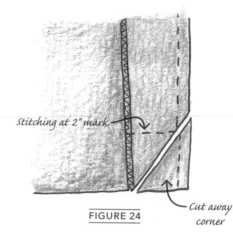

Stitching at 2" mark

FIGURE 24

Cut away corner

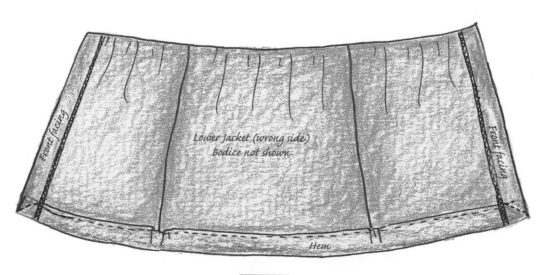

Front facing

Lower Jacket (wrong side) Bodice not shown

Front facing

Hem

FIGURE 25

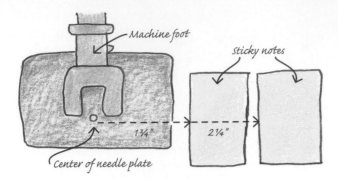

Machine foot

Center of needle plate

Sticky notes

1¾"

2¼"

FIGURE 26

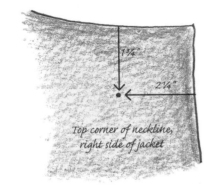

1¾"

2¼"

Top corner of neckline,
right side of jacket

FIGURE 27

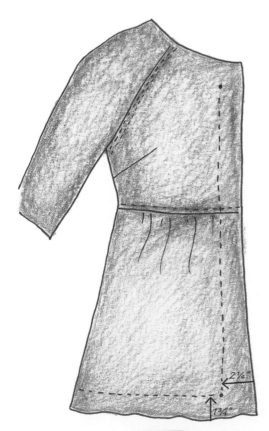

2¼"

1¾"

FIGURE 28

1. To complete the topstitching for the jacket (with or without the collar), you need to place some seam guides on the flatbed of your machine so that the stitching will be much easier to accomplish. I do this by placing sticky notes at certain intervals, eliminating the need to mark the fabric or constantly follow a ruler while stitching.

2. To complete this stitching, you will need to mark 1¾" and 2¼" from the needle on your machine. I start with the largest measurement and place a note at that spot and then place a different note for the smaller measurement. (figure 26)

3. Begin topstitching the jacket through all thicknesses starting at the right front neckline. If your jacket has a collar, start at the neckline seam. If your jacket does *not* have a collar, drop down 1¾" from the neckline seam, as you will be stitching the facing along the neck in place. (figure 27)

4. Stitch down the jackets right front edge, 2¼" from the finished edge, stopping 1¾" from the bottom for the hem. Leave the needle down in the fabric and pivot the jacket. Stitch along the hem 1¾" from the edge. (figure 28)

5. Continue sewing across the bottom of the jacket, stopping 2¼" from the front left edge. Pivot the jacket once more and stitch up the left front edge. If your jacket has a collar, stop at the neckline seam at the top of the jacket. If your jacket does *not* have a collar, stop within 1¾" of the neckline, pivot, and stitch 1¾" from the neckline edge until you reach the original starting point of the stitching. (figure 29)

6. Once this stitching is complete, edgestitch the front finished edges of the jacket as well as the lower hemmed edge. Press.

- - - - ADD THE JACKET BUTTONS - - - -

See your specific project for creating tab closures.

1. Lay the jacket out on a flat surface. Overlap the front edges of the jacket by 1½", with the right front on top of the left front. (figure 30)

2. Lay the buttons on the bodice section between the topstitching and the edge. Space the buttons evenly and measure the distance between them to ensure they are spaced correctly. Mark the position of the buttons. (figure 31)

3. Mark to either side of the buttons for horizontal buttonholes. Stitch the buttonholes and carefully cut each one open.

4. Lay the jacket back on a flat surface with the appropriate overlap and use a chalk pencil to mark through the center of each buttonhole onto the left front for button placement.

5. Check to be sure that the markings for the buttonholes are centered evenly between the buttonhole stitching on the left front, then sew on the buttons. If the buttons are the shank type (no visible holes from the top), sew the buttons on by hand. If the buttons are flat (holes are visible from the top), you can drop the feed dogs on your machine and use a wide zigzag stitch to attach them, taking care so as not to break the buttons or the needle.

- - - - - FINISH THE SLEEVE HEM - - - - -

See your specific project for finishing the sleeve edge. All sleeves have a different hem or edge finish.

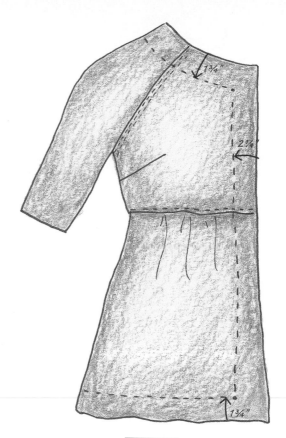

FIGURE 29

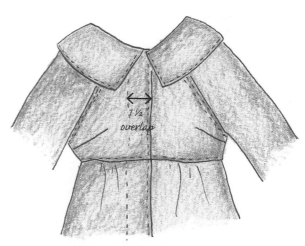

FIGURE 30

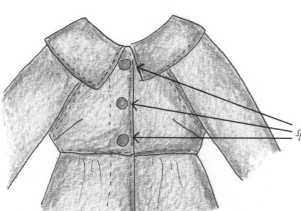

Space buttons an equal distance apart

FIGURE 31

SILK AND LINEN JACKET

Materials list

Main Fabric (all jacket pieces, including the Collar):

All sizes: 3 yards (45"-wide fabric) or 2½ yards (54"-wide fabric)

Contrast Fabric (cuffs, ruffle trim, and silk roses):

All sizes: 1 yard (45"-wide fabric or ¾ yard 54"-wide fabric)

Other Supplies

1¼ yards of 20"-wide fusible interfacing for light- to medium-weight fabrics

Four ⅞"-wide buttons

Polyester machine thread to match fabrics

Rotary cutter, ruler and mat (optional)

Scissors

Chalk pencil

Machine ruffler attachment (optional)

THE SILK AND LINEN JACKET is a hip-length jacket made from hand-overdyed linen and trimmed with silk. It features feminine detailing of silk roses at the sleeve centers and at the center back bodice seam. The silk cuffs and collar overlay give the jacket a dressy feel, perfect for an afternoon wedding or tea with friends. I chose linen for its airy quality and the silk to spice things up a bit. This jacket is short enough that it can be made from a variety of lighter weight fabrics, so if you find a cotton you would like to use, go for it!

MY INITIAL SKETCH

The finished design stayed pretty true to the original sketch—soft, feminine colors with a hint of pink. I love it paired with the ruffled skirt from page 58.

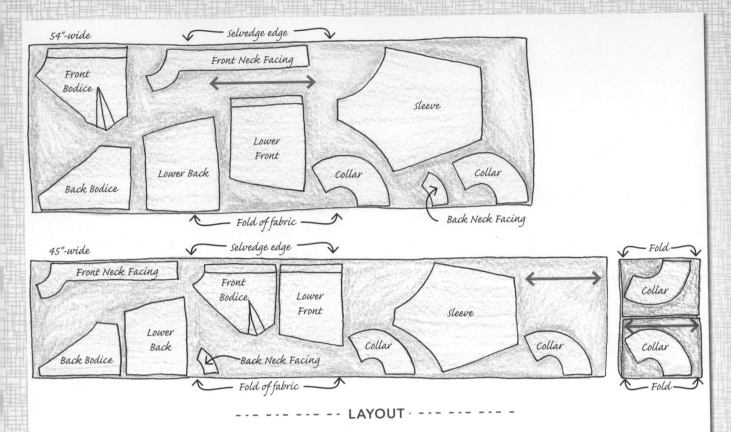

LAYOUT

I've included an illustration showing pattern placement for 54"-wide fabric (a measurement typical for linens) and 45"-wide fabric. From the pattern, use the hip-length cutting line for the Lower Back and Front Neck Facing pieces. Cut all pieces from the main fabric and two additional Collar pieces from the contrast fabric. Note that the layout for the contrast fabric shows that it has been opened up to create two fold lines. This is to conserve fabric for the cuffs and trim. When cutting interfacing for the facing units, cut only *one* piece for the main Collar, and *none* for the Collar overlay. The layout shows how to place the pieces if you're using fabric with a directional print. If there's no apparent direction to the print, then lay the pieces out however best conserves fabric, making sure to follow the grainline.

CONSTRUCTION

1. Follow the instructions in **General Construction** for *Prepare the Facings* and *Create the Collar*. When making the collar, also sew together the Collar overlay from silk, but *do not* interface the silk and use a 1" seam allowance. Trim the seam allowance and finish as for the regular collar. (figure 1)

2. Layer the two finished Collar pieces on top of one another with the right sides facing up. Center the front edges of the smaller Collar piece on top of the main Collar pice and align the inner curved neckline edges. Pin together and sew ⅜" from the edge around the neckline only. (figure 2)

3. Continue with the instructions in **General Construction** for *Make the Front Bodice Darts* and *Sew the Bodice Together*.

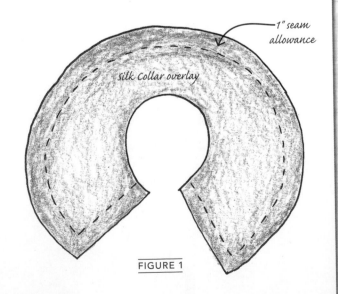

FIGURE 1

- - - - RUFFLE FOR LOWER JACKET - - - -

1. Complete steps 1 and 2 in **General Construction** under *Sew the Lower Jacket Together.*

2. Cut a 3"-wide strip by the width of the fabric from the contrast fabric for the ruffle between the bodice and lower jacket.

3. Fold the strip lengthwise, wrong sides together, and press.

4. With right sides together, pin the ruffle strip to the top edge of the lower jacket matching the raw edges. Sew together with a ¼" seam allowance. (figure 3)

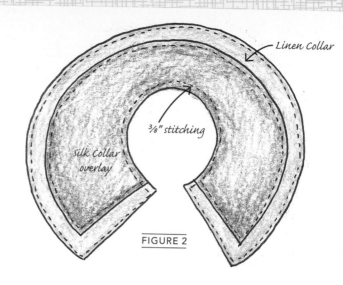

Linen Collar

⅜" stitching

Silk Collar overlay

FIGURE 2

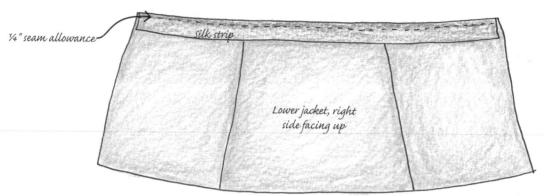

¼" seam allowance

silk strip

Lower jacket, right side facing up

FIGURE 3

COMPLETE THE JACKET CONSTRUCTION

Complete all of the remaining steps in **General Construction**, starting with step 3 in *Sew the Lower Jacket Together,* continuing through *Add the Jacket Buttons.*

Measure sleeve, then add 6" to measurement

FIGURE 4

Cuff, right sides together

9"

FIGURE 5

- - - - - - - SLEEVE CUFFS - - - - - - -

1. Try on the jacket to check the sleeve length. Note that adding the cuff to the jacket will add about 4" to the overall length. If you would like to trim some of the sleeve to retain the three-quarter length, do it at this time.

2. Once the sleeve has been trimmed, measure across the bottom and double this number to get the full circumference of the sleeve. Add 6" to this measurement to allow for the seam allowance and gathering the ruffle for the cuff. (figure 4)

3. Cut two rectangles 9" wide by the measurement determined in the previous step.

4. Fold the cuff strip in half, right sides together, and sew along the 9" edge. Press the seam to one side. (figure 5)

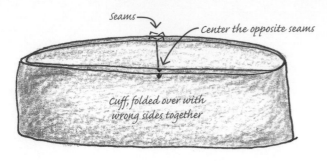

seams

Center the opposite seams

Cuff, folded over with wrong sides together

FIGURE 6

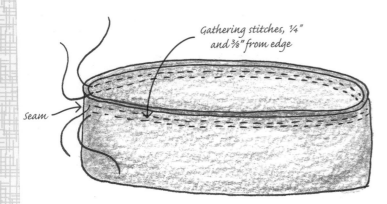

Gathering stitches, ¼" and ⅜" from edge

Seam

FIGURE 7

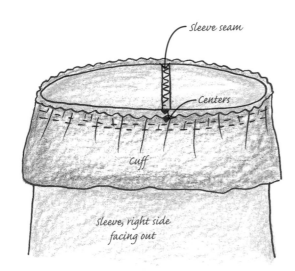

Sleeve seam

Centers

Cuff

Sleeve, right side facing out

FIGURE 8

5. With wrong sides together, fold the cuff in half matching the raw edges.

6. Lay the cuff flat with the seam at one side and snip along the raw edge opposite the seam to mark the center of the cuff. (figure 6)

7. Use a long, straight stitch to sew two rows of stitching from the raw edges of the cuff, one at ¼" and one at ⅜", starting and ending at the seam. (figure 7)

8. Mark the center of the sleeve opposite the sleeve seam as you did for the cuff in step 6. Place the cuff over the right side of the sleeve with raw edges even, matching the seams and center markings. Gently pull the gathering threads until the cuff matches the sleeve width. Distribute gathers evenly and pin in place. (figure 8)

9. Stitch the cuff and sleeve together with a ½" seam allowance. Serge the seam, or trim and use the zigzag to finish the edges. Open the cuff away from the sleeve and press the seam toward the sleeve. Edgestitch the seam on top of the sleeve fabric close to the seam line. (figure 9)

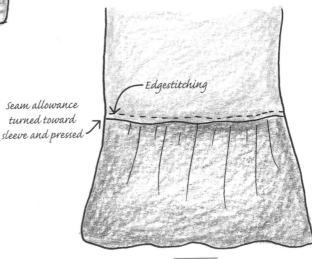

Edgestitching

Seam allowance turned toward sleeve and pressed

FIGURE 9

- - - -- - --- - ROSES - --- - -- - - -

1. To make the roses, cut three 2" by 27" strips from the contrast fabric.

2. Fold each strip in half lengthwise, wrong sides together, matching raw edges; press.

3. Use a long, straight stitch to sew two rows, one at ¼" and one at ⅜" from the raw edges. Create gathers by pulling on the bobbin threads. Or use a ruffler attachment to gather each strip at every stitch, sewing along the long raw edges approximately ¼" from the edge. Press flat.

4. Thread a hand-sewing needle with matching thread and knot. Begin at one end of a strip and fold down the corner diagonally toward the raw gathered edge. Secure with needle and thread, and trim off the corner. (figure 10)

5. Continue rolling up the strip, taking stitches along raw edges as needed to secure the layers. Finish by turning in the remaining end diagonally toward the inside of the flower and stitch in place. Trim off the corner after securing. (figure 11) Repeat for the remaining strips to make three roses.

6. Stitch or pin the roses in place centered on each sleeve opposite the seam just above the ruffle cuff (figure 12) and at the center back at the bodice/lower jacket seam (figure 13).

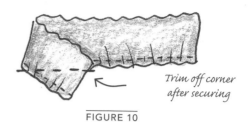

Trim off corner after securing

FIGURE 10

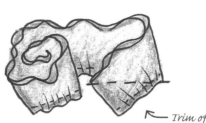

Trim off corner after securing

FIGURE 11

Place rose opposite sleeve seam

FIGURE 12

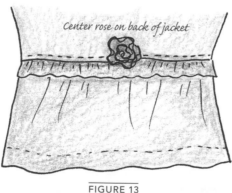

Center rose on back of jacket

FIGURE 13

make it your own

To make this design uniquely your own, play with the fabrics. Maybe you would rather have the cuffs made from linen too. If so, be sure to add about ¼ yard for that variation. You could also make more roses and add them to a matching skirt or cluster them on the jacket at the sleeves and center back, or you could make an extra large one and add it to the collar.

PARISIAN JACKET

Materials list

Main Fabric (All jacket pieces):

All sizes: 2½ yards (45"-wide fabric) or 2 yards (60"-wide fabric)

Other Supplies

1 yard of 20"-wide fusible interfacing for light- to mid-weight fabrics

Six 1"-wide buttons (front tab closure and back button tab)

Four ¾"-wide buttons (sleeve tabs)

Polyester machine thread to match fabrics

Chalk pencil

Hand-sewing needle

Rotary cutter, ruler and mat (optional)

Scissors

THIS HIP-LENGTH JACKET is aptly named the Parisian Jacket, as once it was finished, it reminded me of Paris and the Chanel style. I guess it was the way the fabric came together along with the button tabs! The fabric used for this project is a medium-weight soft woven cotton. I used the wrong side of the fabric for the button closures, because the reversed pattern added a perfect touch. Look closely at both sides of fabric when you shop. You never know when you may find something special like that to use in a design!

MY INITIAL SKETCH

This jacket makes a sophisticated statement when paired with the Appliqué Skirt on page 36.

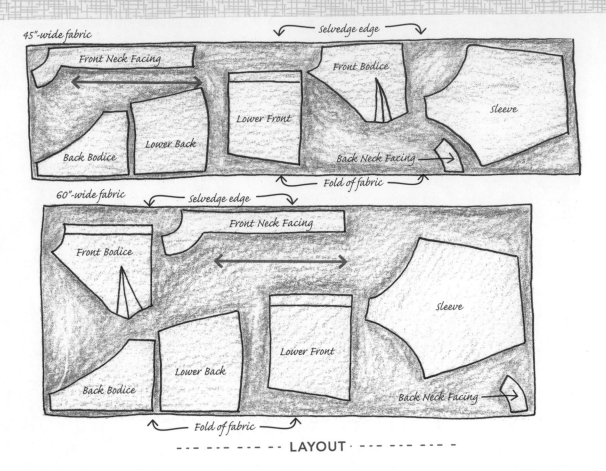

Front Neck Facing

Front Bodice

Sleeve

Lower Front

Back Bodice

Lower Back

Back Neck Facing

Selvedge edge

Fold of fabric

60"-wide fabric

Selvedge edge

Front Neck Facing

Front Bodice

Sleeve

Back Bodice

Lower Back

Lower Front

Back Neck Facing

Fold of fabric

· - - · - - · - - · LAYOUT · - - · - - · - - ·

I've included an illustration showing pattern placement for 60"-wide fabric, as well as 45"-wide fabric. From the pattern, use the hip-length line on the Lower Front, Lower Back and Front Neck Facing pieces. Cut all pieces from the main fabric, including the tabs (not pictured on layout). Also cut facing pieces from the interfacing. Use the open areas of fabric on the layout to position the pieces for the button tabs; cut the quantity as directed on pattern piece. Note that the layout is shown with all pieces going the same way for fabric with a directional pattern. If there is no apparent direction to the print, then pieces can be laid out in either direction to conserve fabric, making sure to follow the grainline.

- - · - - · - - CONSTRUCTION · - - · - - · - -

1. Follow the instructions as written in the **General Construction**, starting with *Prepare the Facings*. Skip the section regarding the collar.

2. After edgestitching the sleeve seams on the bodice, stitch again ¼" from the edgestitching.

3. Continue with the *Make the Front Bodice Dart* section through step 8 of *Sew the Lower Jacket Together* in **General Construction**. Topstitch ¼" away from the edgestitching along bodice/lower jacket seam.

4. Skip *Add the Collar*. Complete all of the steps in *Add the Facings* through *Topstitch the Hem*.

5. Add an additional line of stitching ¼" to the inside of the stitching holding the facings and hem in place.

6. Clean-finish the sleeves on the serger or with a zigzag stitch and turn up a 2" hem. Press. Stitch 1¾" from the pressed edge and again ¼" away. Edgestitch the pressed edge of the sleeve as well. (figure 1)

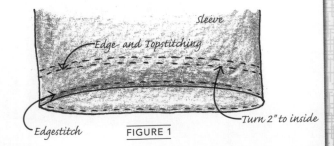

Sleeve

Edge- and Topstitching

Edgestitch

Turn 2" to inside

FIGURE 1

- - - - - BUTTON TABS & CLOSURE - - - - -

1. Apply interfacing following the manufacturer's instructions to the wrong side of the following pieces: two of the Front Button Tabs, one of the Back Button Tabs, and two of the Sleeve Tabs.

2. Pin one interfaced piece to a non-interfaced piece, right sides together, matching the edges.

3. Sew all tabs together with a ¼" seam allowance, leaving an opening along one of the long sides for turning. (figure 2)

4. Turn the tabs right side out and press, turning in the open edges. Edgestitch each tab piece. (figure 3)

5. Lay the jacket on a flat surface and overlap the jacket fronts by 1½", right side over left side. Place the first Front Button Tab in line with the decorative stitching lines below the neckline. Center the Front Button Tab extending 2" beyond the right front edge onto the left front. (figure 4)

6. Position the other Front Button Tab 1½" above the bodice seam, also centered as before. Using a chalk pencil, mark the placement of both Front Button Tabs on the jacket at the top, bottom and sides points. (figure 5)

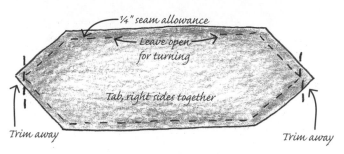

¼" seam allowance
Leave open for turning
Tab, right sides together
Trim away   Trim away

FIGURE 2

Edgestitching
Tab, right sides together

FIGURE 3

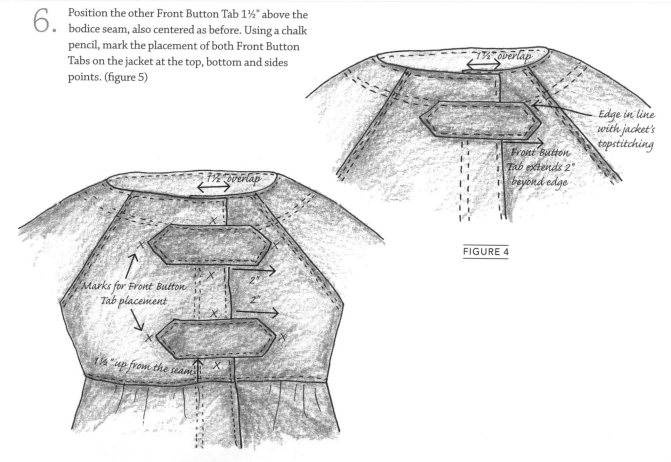

1½" overlap
Edge in line with jacket's topstitching
Front Button Tab extends 2" beyond edge

FIGURE 4

1½" overlap
Marks for Front Button Tab placement
2"
2"
1½" up from the seam

FIGURE 5

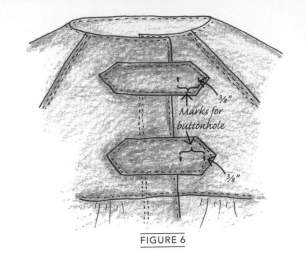

FIGURE 6

7. Lay the buttons onto the Front Button Tabs along the side that extends onto the left front, about ⅜" in from the outer point. Using a chalk pencil, mark either side of the button for a horizontal buttonhole. Only mark for the buttonholes on this side of each Front Button Tab. (figure 6)

8. Remove the Front Button Tabs from the jacket and make the buttonholes. Cut the buttonholes open and reposition the Front Button Tabs onto the jacket front, with the buttonhole side extending off of the right front of the jacket, over the left front.

9. Edgestitch the Front Button Tab onto the right front of the jacket along all edges where they touch. (figure 7)

10. Overlap the jacket fronts and mark the button placement on the left front. Hand-sew the buttons in place. Add the remaining buttons to the Front Button Tabs, making sure that they line up with the other buttons.

11. Center the Sleeve Tabs on each sleeve opposite the seam and in line with the stitching that holds the hem in place. Pin the Sleeve Tabs in place. Center the buttons about ⅜" in from each end and hand-sew through all layers to secure both the tab and the buttons. (figure 8)

12. Center the Back Button Tab directly over the jacket's Back Bodice and Lower Back seam. Pin in place. Stitch the ends of the Back Button Tab in place as shown in the diagram. Sew the buttons to the Back Button Tab, about ⅜" in from each end and centered vertically. (figure 9)

Begin and end edgestitching at the edge of the jacket's right front

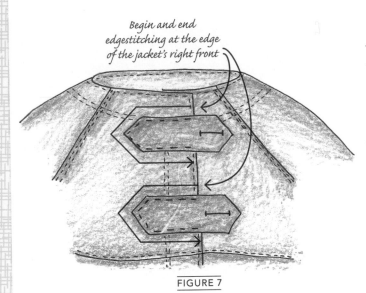

FIGURE 7

Sleeve Tab centered opposite sleeve seam

Lower edge in line with sleeve's topstitching

Sleeve seam

Buttons hold the tab in place

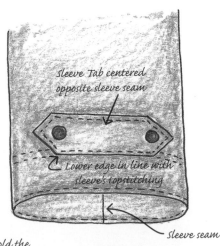

FIGURE 8

Back of jacket

Back Button Tab centered over bodice seam

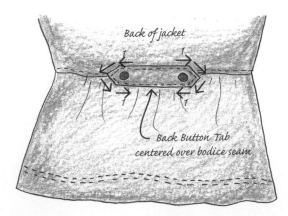

FIGURE 9

make it your own

Make this jacket your own by changing up the contrast for the button tabs. If you can't find a fabric that is truly reversible, consider using wool for the tabs or some other textured fabric. You could also use two coordinating fabrics; one for the jacket and the other for the button tabs. Have fun with your button choices. This would be a great place to show off some retro or antique buttons.

COZY WOOL JACKET

Materials list

Main Fabric (all jacket pieces,
   including the Collar):
   All sizes 3½ yards (45"-
   wide fabric) or 3¼ yards
   (54"-wide fabric)

Other Supplies

1½ yards of 20"-wide fusible
   interfacing for light- to
   medium-weight fabrics
Five 1½"-wide covered
   buttons (front closure and
   back button tab)
Six ¾"-wide covered buttons
   (for cuffs and faux
   pocket flaps)
Polyester machine thread to
   match fabrics
Chalk pencil
Hand-sewing needle
Rotary cutter, ruler and mat
   (optional)
Scissors

THE COZY WOOL JACKET is a stylish way to stay warm
on wickedly cold days. The over-dyed wool in a chartreuse
hounds tooth pattern is an eye-catcher, especially with all
of the tailored detailing including large cuffs, faux pocket
flaps, back button tab, and large covered buttons for the
closure and cuffs. This jacket is fingertip-length and will
look its best made from a medium- to heavy-weight fabric.
Wool is perfect, but a heavy (yet soft) twill or velveteen
would work nicely here also.

MY INITIAL SKETCH

I had this lovely chartreuse wool in mind when I sketched the
jacket. Rather than using a contrasting fabric for the added
elements (the faux pocket flaps, oversized cuffs and covered
buttons), I splurged and used more of the hand-dyed wool. This
jacket is great paired with the Flirty Tunic Dress (page 100)

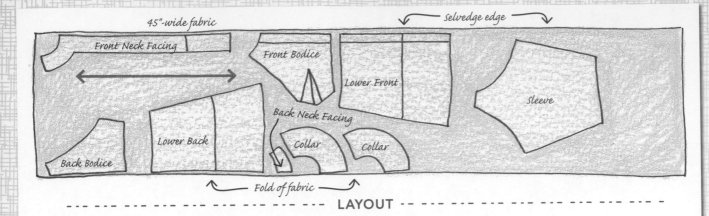

Selvedge edge

Front Neck Facing

Front Bodice

Lower Front

Sleeve

Lower Back

Back Neck Facing

Collar

Collar

Back Bodice

45"-wide fabric

Fold of fabric

LAYOUT

Use the fingertip-length cutting line on the Lower Back, Lower Front and Front Neck Facing pieces. Cut all pieces from the main fabric. Position the pieces for the Back Button Tab and Faux Pocket Flaps on the open areas of the layout; cut the quantity as directed by the pattern piece. Cut Front Neck Facing, Back Neck Facing and Collar pieces from interfacing; save the scraps for the Back Button Tab, Faux Pocket Flaps and covered buttons. Note that the layout is shown with all pieces going the same way for fabric with a directional pattern. If there is no apparent direction to the fabric, then pieces can be laid out in either direction to conserve fabric, making sure to follow the grainline.

CONSTRUCTION

Complete *all* of the steps in the **General Construction**. Take note that the collar edges have been double topstitched. Everything else is edgestitched only.

If you're not using a thick fabric like wool and are covering buttons, fuse scraps of interfacing to the wrong side of the fabric; this will prevent the metal of the button form from showing through.

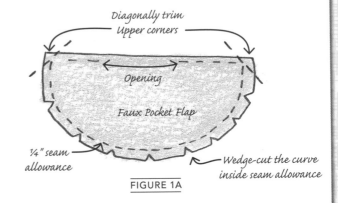

Diagonally trim
Upper corners

Opening

Faux Pocket Flap

¼" seam allowance

Wedge-cut the curve inside seam allowance

FIGURE 1A

ADD FAUX POCKET FLAPS AND BACK BUTTON TAB

1. Add interfacing to the wrong side of two Faux Pocket Flaps and one Back Button Tab.

2. Pin one interfaced piece with a non-interfaced piece, right sides together, matching the edges.

3. Sew all pieces together with a ¼" seam allowance, leaving an opening along one of the long sides for turning. (figures 1a, 1b)

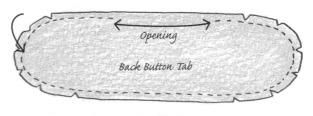

Wedge-cut the curve
inside seam allowance

Opening

Back Button Tab

FIGURE 1B

working with wool

If you choose to make this jacket from wool, you won't need to finish the seams. Instead, you can simply press open all of the interior seams, and then edgestitch to either side of the seam.

4. Turn the tab and pocket flaps right side out and press, turning in the open edges. Edgestitch around each piece. (figure 2a, 2b)

5. Lay the jacket on a flat surface and overlap the jacket fronts by 1½", right side over left side. Lay the pocket flaps with their top edge even with the bodice seam. Center the flaps between the side seams and jacket front edges.

6. Pin the flaps in place and edgestitch along the top edge over the previous row of stitching. (figure 3)

7. Hand-sew a ¾" covered button to each pocket flap through all layers.

8. Center the back button tab along the center back of the jacket at the bodice seam. Center from side to side and directly over the seam; pin in place. Stitch the tab in place starting 2" in from the end along the top and following the curve around the end to 2" in at the bottom, following the previous edgestitching. Repeat for the other end. Hand-sew through all layers 1½" buttons to either end of the tab. (figure 4)

– – – – – – SLEEVE CUFFS – – – – – –

1. Try on the jacket to check the sleeve length. Note that adding the cuff to the jacket will add about 1" to the overall sleeve length. If you would like to trim away a bit of the sleeve to retain the length at three-quarters, do it at this time.

2. Once the sleeve has been trimmed, measure around the bottom edge to get the full circumference of the sleeve. Add 1" to this measurement for the seam allowance. (figure 5)

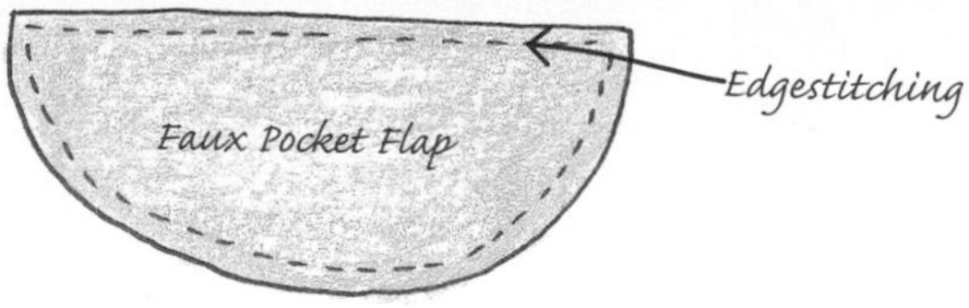

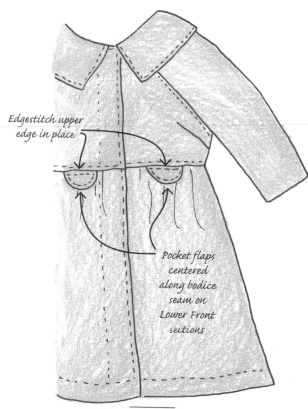

Faux Pocket Flap — Edgestitching

FIGURE 2A

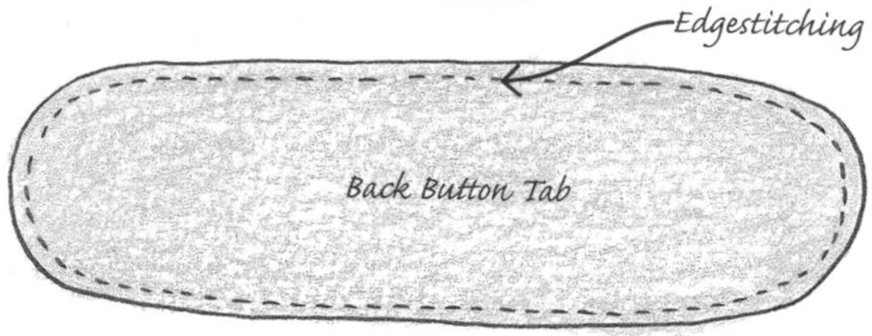

Edgestitching

Back Button Tab

FIGURE 2B

Edgestitch upper edge in place

Pocket flaps centered along bodice seam on Lower Front sections

FIGURE 3

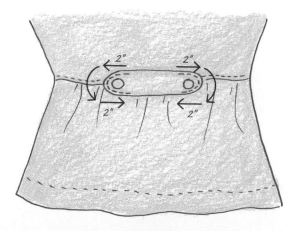

2"   2"
2"   2"

FIGURE 4

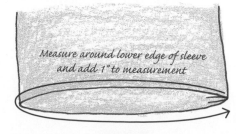

Measure around lower edge of sleeve and add 1" to measurement

FIGURE 5

137

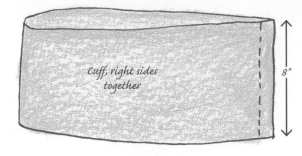

FIGURE 6

Cuff, right sides together

8"

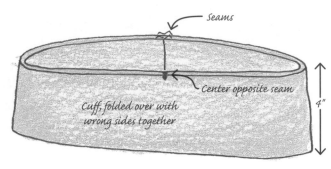

Seams

Center opposite seam

Cuff, folded over with wrong sides together

4"

FIGURE 7

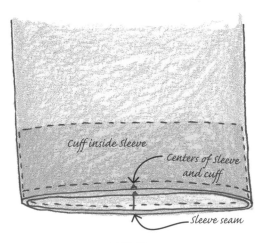

Cuff inside sleeve

Centers of sleeve and cuff

Sleeve seam

FIGURE 8

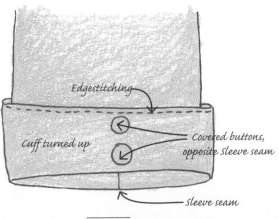

Edgestitching

Cuff turned up

Covered buttons, opposite sleeve seam

Sleeve seam

FIGURE 9

3. Cut two rectangles 8"-wide by the measurement determined in the previous step for cuffs.

4. Fold each cuff in half, right sides together, and sew along the 8" edge. Press the seam to one side, or, if sewing with wool, press open. (figure 6)

5. With wrong sides together and seams even, fold each cuff in half, matching the raw edges.

6. Find the center of each cuff piece and snip the raw edges opposite the seam line. (figure 7)

7. Find the center of the sleeve opposite the seam and mark it, as you did for the cuff in step 6. With the right side of the cuff against the wrong side of the sleeve, match the seamlines and center marks. Pin in place and stitch. (figure 8)

8. Trim the seam. Open the cuff away from the sleeve and press the seam toward the sleeve. Fold up the cuff so that it's about 3" deep and press. Open the cuff away from the sleeve again and edgestitch around the cuff. Fold back into place.

9. Hand-sew two ¾" covered buttons to the center of each cuff opposite the seam. (figure 9)

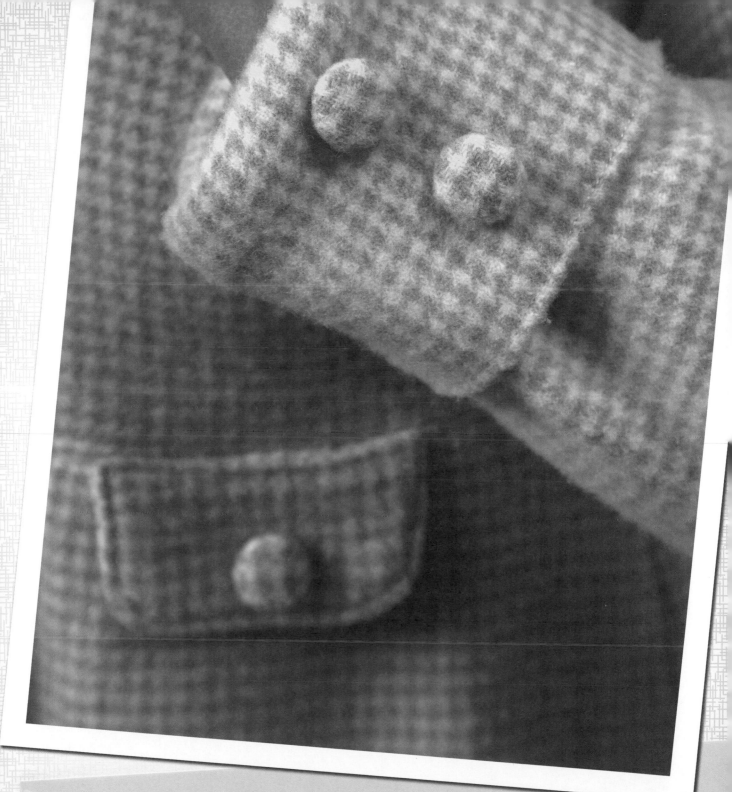

make it your own

Make this design your own by using a wide-wale corduroy or velveteen fabric. Even a large plaid wool would be great here. I can even see a mix of these fabrics on one jacket for a Bohemian look… Top it off with a pretty scarf and off you go!

DENIM AND FAUX FUR JACKET

THE DENIM AND FAUX FUR JACKET is a fun fingertip-length jacket with patch pockets and an oversized crazy collar and cuffs. I washed and dried the fur for this jacket several times to give it that "extra ratty" look. I also washed and dried the denim for this jacket a couple of times to be sure that the dye was stable and the denim was softened. The denim used for this jacket is actually a Tencel/denim blend, giving it wonderful drape, much like rayon, but heavier. I highly recommend this blend. It makes the jacket feel more luxurious and the drape is divine!

MY INITIAL SKETCH

I wanted a fun and funky feel to this design, and I think the ratty fur and large patch pockets do the trick. I like pairing this jacket with the Ruffle Trimmed Tunic (page 84).

Materials list

Main Fabric (all jacket pieces, including one Collar piece):
All sizes: 3⅛ yards (60"-wide fabric)
Faux Fur (on Collar pieces and cuffs):
All sizes: ½ yard

Other Supplies

1½ yards of 20"-wide fusible interfacing for light- to medium-weight fabrics
Four 1"-wide buttons (front closure)
Polyester machine thread to match fabrics (if making jacket from denim, use thread specifically for denim fabrics)
Chalk pencil
Rotary cutter, ruler and mat (optional)
Scissors

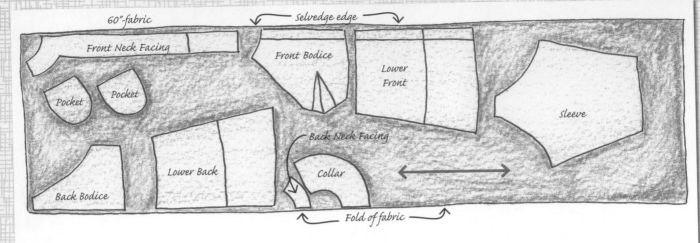

Use the fingertip-length cutting line on the Lower Back, Lower Front and Front Neck Facing pieces. Cut all pieces from the main fabric. Cut one Collar piece from the fur. Cut facing and Collar pieces from interfacing; save the scraps for the Pocket pieces. The layout above shows how to place all the pieces if you're using fabric with a directional print. If there is no apparent direction to the print, then lay the pieces out however best conserves fabric, making sure to follow the grainline.

CONSTRUCTION · --- --- -

1. Complete all of the steps in **General Construction**, starting with *Prepare the Facings* all the way through to the *Finish the Sleeve Hem*.

2. For the collar, interface the denim Collar piece and use it as an undercollar for the faux fur Collar piece. This way, you are not dealing with two layers of fur, which would be bulky and never lay correctly.

3. Double topstitch all of the seams.

4. Add an additional line of stitching ¼ inside of the stitching holding the facings and hem in place. (figure 1)

Additional line of stitching

FIGURE 1

working with faux fur

When working with faux fur, be prepared for a mess because the fabric loves to shed. A sticky lint roller is extremely helpful when working with faux fur. When laying out the Collar piece, follow the direction of the fur on the grainline. Push the pile away from the cutting line as you cut, so you don't accidently trim the pile unevenly. In order to reduce bulk when sewing seams, trim the pile of the fur very close to the backing within the seam allowance. It helps the seams lie flatter when the collar and cuffs are finished. Also remember to keep the heat of the iron away from fur—they do *not* get along!

ADD POCKETS

1. Cut out four Pocket pieces. Interface two of them.

2. Pin one interfaced Pocket piece to one non-interfaced Pocket piece, right sides together, with raw edges even.

3. Sew around the edges using a ¼" seam allowance, leaving an opening along the straight edge for turning. Notch the curves and cut diagonally across the corners. (figure 2)

4. Turn the pockets right side out and press, turning the opening to the inside and pressing. Double topstitch the straight edge of the pocket. (figure 3)

5. Add the pockets to the Lower Front portion of the jacket with the top edges angled. Center the pockets and pin in place, checking to be sure that they are at the same position on each side. Try on the jacket to check the placement and make any adjustments as necessary.

6. When you're pleased with the placement, double topstitch the pockets in place around the curved edges only. (figure 5)

CREATE SLEEVE CUFFS

1. Try on the jacket to check the sleeve length. Note that adding the cuff to the jacket will add about 3" to the overall length. If you would like to trim away some of the sleeve to retain the three-quarters length, do it at this time. If you would like full-length sleeves, leave the sleeve length as is.

2. Measure around the bottom end of the sleeve to get the full circumference of the sleeve. Add 1" to this measurement to allow for the seam allowance. (figure 5)

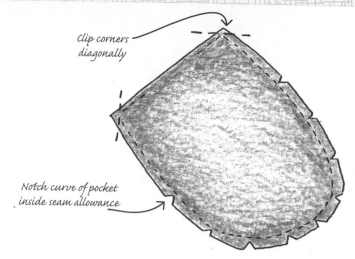

Clip corners diagonally

Notch curve of pocket inside seam allowance

FIGURE 2

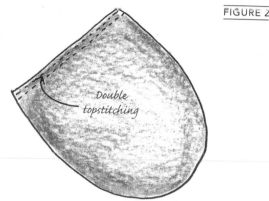

Double topstitching

FIGURE 3

Double topstitch curved edges of pockets

FIGURE 4

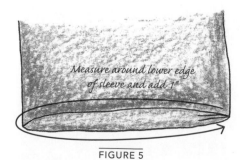

Measure around lower edge of sleeve and add 1"

FIGURE 5

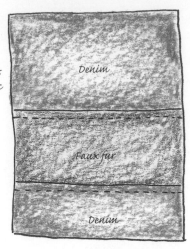

Wrong sides
of the fabric

Denim

Faux fur

Denim

FIGURE 6

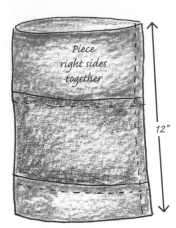

Piece
right sides
together

12"

FIGURE 7

3. Cut four rectangles from denim, two 6½"-wide and two 2½"-wide by the measurement determined in step 2. Also cut two pieces of faux fur, 5"-wide (going with the pile of the fur) by the measurement determined from step 2.

4. With the right sides together, pin the narrower denim piece to a long side of the faux fur. Pin the wider denim piece to the opposite fur edge. Sew both seams with a ½" seam allowance. Repeat for the other cuff. (figure 6)

5. Fold the cuff in half, right sides together, matching seams, and sew along the 12" edge. Carefully press the seam to one side. (figure 7)

6. Turn the cuff, right side out, and fold in half with wrong sides together and raw edges even. The large denim rectangle will be completely to the inside of the cuff. (figure 8)

7. Lay the cuff flat with the seam along one side and snip along the raw edge opposite the seam to mark the center of the cuff.

8. Find the center of the sleeve opposite the sleeve seam, in the same manner as the cuff in the previous step. With the cuff wrong side out, fur to the inside, and the sleeve wrong side out, slip the cuff inside the sleeve and match the center markings and seams. Pin the pieces together and sew around the edges with a ½" seam allowance. Trim the seam and finish the edge with a serger or a zigzag stitch. (figure 9)

9. Turn the sleeve, right side out, and open the cuff. Before turning the cuff up, only denim should be showing at this point. Press the cuff seam, using a pressing cloth to protect the faux fur. Turn the cuff up so the fur is facing the outside of the jacket and almost all of the fur is exposed. The edge of the fur should just align with the seam, concealing it.

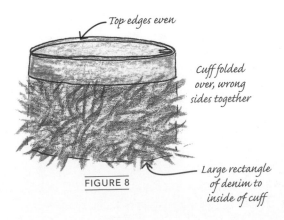

Top edges even

Cuff folded
over, wrong
sides together

Large rectangle
of denim to
inside of cuff

FIGURE 8

FIGURE 9

make it your own

Make this jacket your own by choosing a different fabric. A nice sun-washed canvas-type fabric would make a great jacket, especially with a soft shearling-like fur at the collar and cuffs.

MOD JACKET

Materials list

Main Fabric (all jacket
   pieces):
   All sizes: 3½ yards (45"-
   wide fabric) or 3½ yards
   (60"-wide fabric)
Contrast Fabric (belt and
   button tabs):
   All sizes: ¾ yard (45"-wide
   fabric) or ⅝ yard
   (60"-wide fabric)

Other Supplies

1¾ yards of 20"-wide fusible
   interfacing for light- to
   medium-weight fabrics
Four 1½"-wide covered
   buttons (front closure)
Polyester machine thread to
   match fabrics
Chalk pencil
Rotary cutter, ruler and mat
   (optional)
Scissors

WEARING THE MOD JACKET is like getting into a time machine and being whisked back to the glorious 1970s! This twill fabric has an abundance of color and pattern, making it perfect for creating its own scene. It would be perfect with jeans and boots. Featuring button front tabs and an oversized tie belt, this jacket is anything but blah! Look for retro prints to make this jacket. A great large-scale retro floral would also make for a wonderful look. Have fun with your fabric choices!

MY INITIAL SKETCH

With this design, I wanted to go all out, seeing how far I could go with an outrageous print. I think it's the perfect blend of mod 1970s and current fashion.

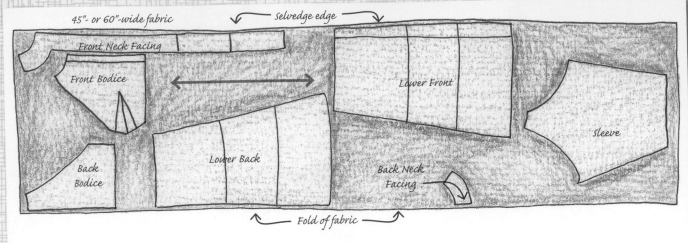

45"- or 60"-wide fabric

Selvedge edge

Front Neck Facing

Front Bodice

Lower Front

Sleeve

Back Bodice

Lower Back

Back Neck Facing

Fold of fabric

LAYOUT

Use the knee-length cutting line on the Lower Front, Lower Back and Front Neck Facing pieces. Cut all pieces from the main fabric, except for the Front Button Tabs and tie belt (these will be cut from the contrast fabric). Cut facing pieces from interfacing; save the scraps for the Front Button Tabs and tie belt. The layout above shows how to place the pieces if you're using fabric with a directional print. If there is no apparent direction to the print, then lay the pieces out however best conserves fabric, making sure to follow grainlines.

CONSTRUCTION

1. Follow the instructions as written in the **General Construction**, starting with *Prepare the Facings*. Skip the section regarding the collar.

2. After edgestitching the sleeve seams on the bodice, stitch again ¼" from the edgestitching.

3. Continue with the *Make the Front Bodice Darts* section through step 8 of *Sew the Lower Jacket Together* in **General Construction**. Topstitch ¼" away from edgestitching along the bodice/lower jacket seam.

4. Skip *Add the Collar*. Complete all of the steps in *Add the Facings* through *Topstitch the Hem*.

5. Add an additional line of stitching ¼" to the inside of the stitching holding the facings and hem in place. (figure 1)

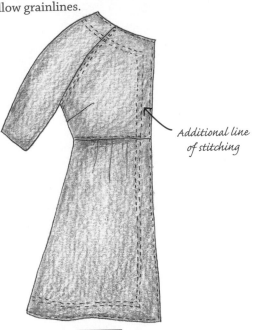

Additional line of stitching

FIGURE 1

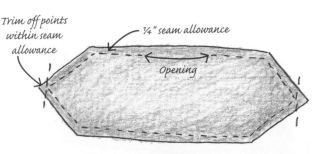

Trim off points within seam allowance

¼" seam allowance

Opening

FIGURE 2

BUTTON TAB CLOSURE

1. Apply interfacing to the wrong side of two of the Front Button Tab pieces.

2. Pin one interfaced piece to a non-interfaced piece, right sides together, matching the raw edges.

3. Sew all tabs with right sides together and a ¼" seam allowance. Leave an opening along one of the long sides for turning. (figure 2)

4. Turn the tabs right side out and press, turning in the open edges. Edgestitch each tab piece. (figure 3)

5. Lay the jacket on a flat surface and overlap the jacket fronts, right front over the left front, by about 1½". Place the first Front Button Tab in line with the stitching lines below the neckline. Center the Front Button Tab so that it extends 2" beyond the right front edge onto the left front. (figure 4)

6. Position the remaining front Front Button Tab about 2" below the lower edge of the upper tab. Using a chalk pencil, mark the placement of the Front Button Tabs at the top edge, bottom edge and side points. (figure 5)

7. Lay the buttons onto the Front Button Tab along the side that extends onto the left front, about ⅜" in from the outer point and mark either side of the button for a horizontal buttonhole. Only mark for buttonholes on this side of each Front Button Tab. (figure 6)

8. Remove Front Button Tabs from the jacket and make the buttonholes. Cut open the buttonholes and reposition the tabs onto the jacket front, with the buttonhole side extending off the right front of the jacket.

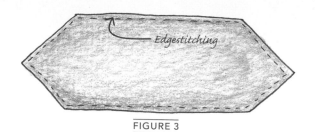
Edgestitching

FIGURE 3

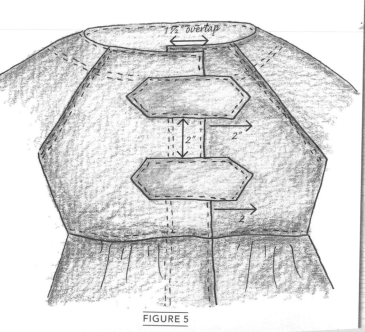

1½" overlap

2"

FIGURE 4

FIGURE 5

1½" overlap

2"

2"

2"

2

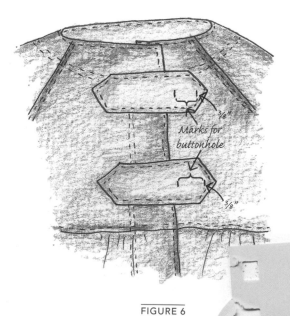

⅜"

Marks for buttonhole

⅜"

FIGURE 6

working with covered buttons

If you're covering buttons, fuse scraps of interfacing to the wrong side of the fabric first. This way, the metal button form won't show through.

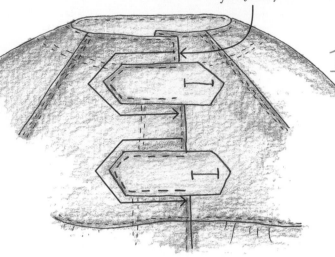

Edgestitch the tab onto the right front, beginning and ending at the edge of the jacket front

FIGURE 7

9. Edgestitch the Front Button Tabs onto the right front of the jacket along all edges where they touch. (figure 7)

10. Overlap the jacket fronts and mark the button placement on the left front. Hand-sew the buttons in place. Add a button to the right side of the Front Button Tabs in line with the button already in place.

- -- -- --- SLEEVE CUFFS - -- -- --- -

1. Try on the jacket to check the sleeve length. Note that adding the cuff to the jacket will add about 3" to the overall sleeve length. If you would like to trim away some of the sleeve to keep the three-quarters length, do it at this time.

2. Once the sleeve has been trimmed, measure around the bottom to get the full circumference of the Sleeve. Add 5" to this measurement to allow for the seam allowance and ruffling the cuff. (figure 8)

3. Cut two rectangles 8" wide by the measurement determined in the previous step.

4. Fold the cuff in half lengthwise, right sides together, and sew along the 8" edge. Press the seam to one side. (figure 9)

5. Turn the cuff, right side out, and fold in half with wrong sides together and raw edges even.

6. Lay the cuff flat with the seam along one side. Snip the raw edge opposite the seam to mark the center of the cuff. (figure 10)

Measure the sleeve, then add 5" to measurement

FIGURE 8

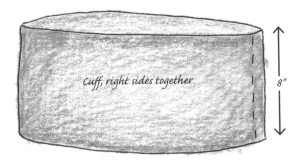

Cuff, right sides together

8"

FIGURE 9

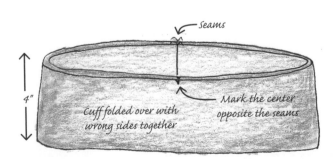

Seams

Cuff folded over with wrong sides together

Mark the center opposite the seams

4"

FIGURE 10

7. Use a long, straight stitch to sew two rows of stitching from the raw edges on the cuff, one at ¼" and one at ⅜", starting and ending at the seam. (figure 11)

8. Mark the center opposite the sleeve seam in the same manner as the cuff. Place the right side of the sleeve inside the cuff with raw edges even, matching the seams and center markings. Pull the gathering threads until the cuff matches the sleeve width. Distribute the gathers evenly and pin in place. (figure 12)

9. Stitch the cuff and sleeve together. Serge the seam or trim the edge and zigzag. Open out the cuff away from the sleeve and press the seam toward the sleeve. Double topstitch the seam on top of the sleeve fabric close to the seamline. (figure 13)

- - - - - - - - - - - - - - TIE BELT - - - - - - - - -

1. Cut 7½"-wide strips by the width of the fabric from the contrast fabric; two from 60" width fabric, or three from 45" width fabric. Trim the selvedges from the ends and piece, right sides together, with a ¼" seam, along the short sides forming one long strip.

2. Cut a series of strips from fusible interfacing, 3¾"-wide to accommodate the length of the belt. When fusing, allow about ¼" overlap of interfacing strips.

3. Apply the interfacing to the wrong side of one half of the belt strip. (figure 14)

4. Fold the strip in half lengthwise, right sides together, and sew along the long edge with a ½" seam allowance, forming a tube.

5. Turn right side out and press with the seam along one side. Double topstitch both long edges of the tie belt.

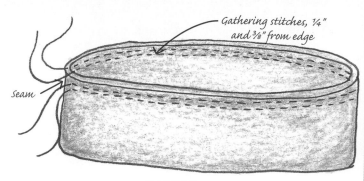

Gathering stitches, ¼" and ⅜" from edge

Seam

FIGURE 11

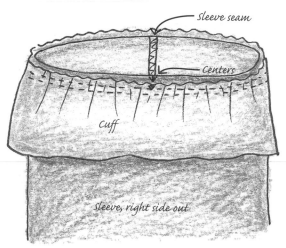

Sleeve seam

Centers

Cuff

Sleeve, right side out

FIGURE 12

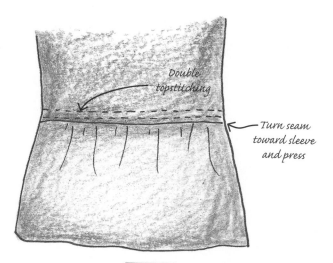

Double topstitching

Turn seam toward sleeve and press

FIGURE 13

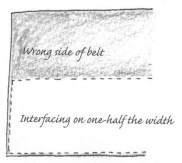

Wrong side of belt

Interfacing on one-half the width

FIGURE 14

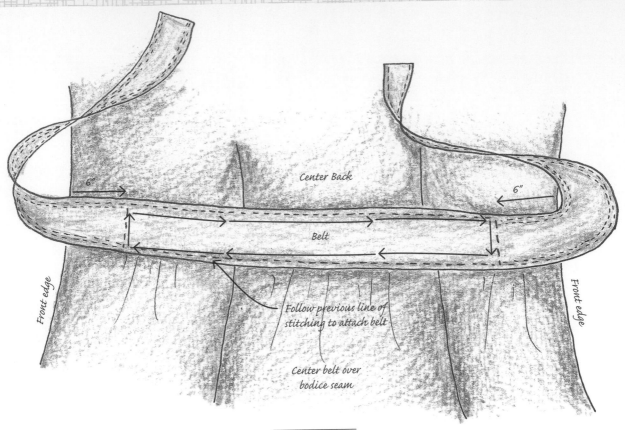

6"

Center Back

Belt

6"

Front edge

Front edge

Follow previous line of stitching to attach belt

Center belt over bodice seam

FIGURE 15, 16, 17

Turn up lower edge of the belt twice, then edgestitch

FIGURE 18

7. Center the belt on the back of the jacket, with the seam of the belt over the bodice seam. Pin the belt in place, starting at the center. (figure 15)

8. Work outward from the center of the back of the jacket to within 6" of the front edges on both sides. (figure 16)

9. Edgestitch the upper edge of the belt in place, stitching over the previous stitching. Start and stop at the 6" marking. (figure 17)

10. Edgestitch the lower edge of the belt in place, stitching over pressed creases. Sew across each end of the belt at the 6" marking.

11. Try on the jacket and tie the belt. Determine how much should be cut away from both ends of the belt and mark.

12. Cut away excess length of belt. Turn up the ends of the belt twice by ¼" and double topstitch in place. (figure 18)

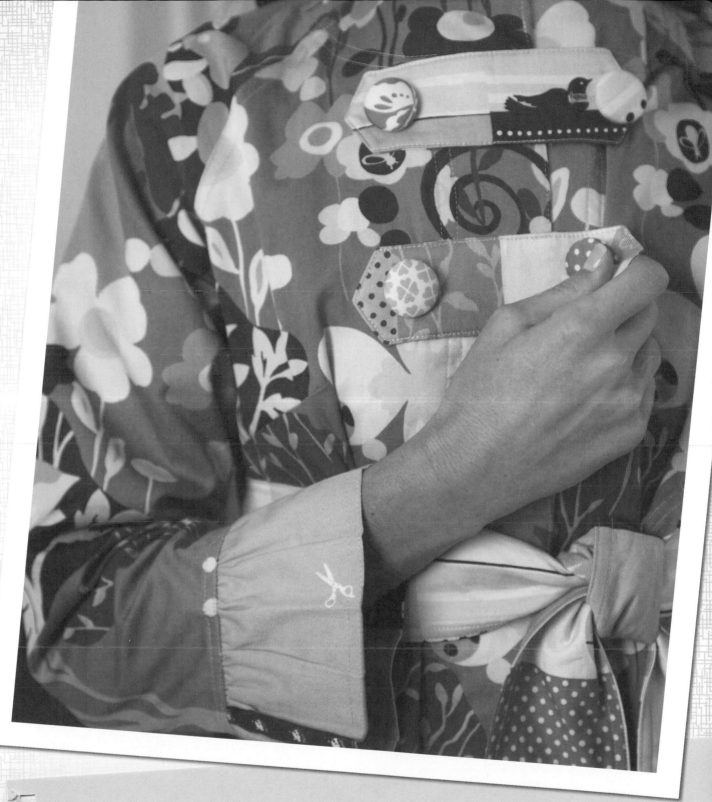

make it your own

Make this jacket your own by adding a special trim to the cuffs or detailing to the belt. Change the cuffs and add one from a different variation. Make it from a solid fabric to totally change the look. Making the cuffs from crushed velvet would be really fun!

CLASSIC TAILORED JACKET

Materials list

Main Fabric (all jacket pieces, including Collar pieces):
All sizes: 4¼ yards (45"-wide fabric) or 3¼ yards (60"-wide fabric)

Other Supplies

1⅝ yards of 20"-wide fusible interfacing for light- to medium-weight fabrics
Six ⅞"-wide buttons (four for front closure, two for collar)
Six ¾"-wide buttons (cuffs)
Polyester machine thread to match fabrics
Chalk pencil
Rotary cutter, ruler and mat (optional)
Scissors

THE CLASSIC TAILORED JACKET has a slight retro feel with the choice of yellow and gray leaf fabric. This is a great, reversible fabric, so notice that the collar and cuffs are the reverse of the rest of the jacket. It's a nice subtle detail. This jacket gets the tailored detailing of double topstitching and a lot of buttons with super long cuffs. This is a knee-length jacket and would look great with a long skirt or a knee-length tunic dress.

MY INITIAL SKETCH

For this jacket, I wanted something cool and sophisticated, yet fun and retro. The gray and yellow is an unexpected but pleasant break from something with higher contrast, like black and white.

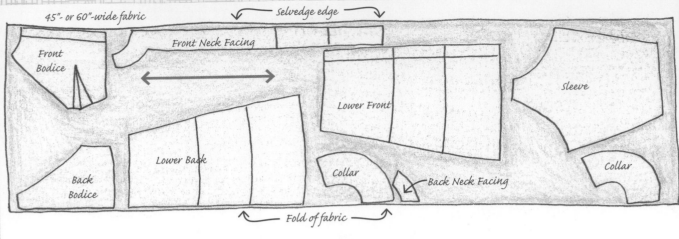

45"- or 60"-wide fabric   selvedge edge

Front Bodice

Front Neck Facing

Lower Front

Sleeve

Lower Back

Collar

Back Neck Facing

Collar

Back Bodice

Fold of fabric

LAYOUT

Use the knee-length cutting line on the Lower Front, Lower Back and Front Neck Facing pieces. Cut all pieces from the main fabric. Note that the layout is shown with all pieces going the same way for fabric with a directional pattern. If there is no apparent direction to the fabric, then pieces can be laid out in either direction to conserve fabric, making sure to follow the grainlines.

CONSTRUCTION

Complete all of the steps in the **General Construction** for this jacket. Take note that the collar edges and sleeve seams have been double topstitched. Everything else is edgestitched only.

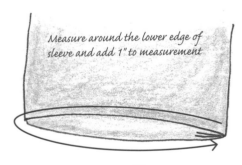

Measure around the lower edge of sleeve and add 1" to measurement

FIGURE 1

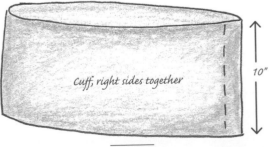

Cuff, right sides together

10"

FIGURE 2

COLLAR BUTTONS

1. Try on the jacket. Pin the front edges of the collar to the bodice fronts so the collar lays naturally.

2. Mark 1" in from the side and front edges of the collar for button placement. (figure 1) Hand-sew buttons at markings through all thicknesses.

SLEEVE CUFFS

1. Try on the jacket to check the sleeve length. Note that adding the cuff to the jacket will add about 4" to the overall length. If you would like to trim away some of the sleeve to keep the three-quarters length, do it at this time.

2. Measure around the bottom of the sleeve to get the full circumference of the sleeve. Add 1" to this measurement to allow for the seam allowance. (figure 2)

3. Cut two rectangles 10" wide by the measurement determined in the previous step. Fold the cuff in half, right sides together, and sew along the 10" edge. Press the seam to one side, or open the seam if sewing with wool. (figure 3)

4. Turn the cuff, right side out, and fold in half with wrong sides together and raw edges and seams even.

5. Lay cuff flat with the seam along one side and snip along the raw edge opposite the seam to mark the center of the cuff. (figure 3)

6. Mark the center opposite the sleeve seam in the same manner as the cuff. Place the sleeve inside the cuff and match the raw edges and center markings. Pin in place and stitch with a ½" seam allowance. (figure 4)

7. Trim the seam and clean-finish with a serger or a zigzag stitch. Open the cuff away from the sleeve and press the seam toward the sleeve. Edgestitch on either side of the seam where the cuff joins the sleeve. Double topstitch the lower edge of the cuff. (figure 5)

8. Hand-sew three ¾" buttons to the center of each cuff opposite the seam. (figure 6)

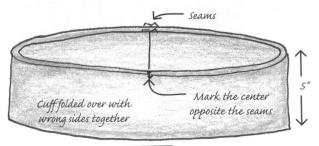

Seams

Cuff folded over with wrong sides together

Mark the center opposite the seams

5"

FIGURE 3

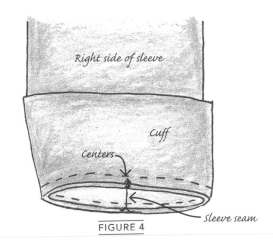

Right side of sleeve

Cuff

Centers

Sleeve seam

FIGURE 4

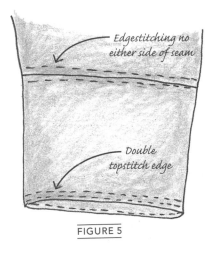

Edgestitching no either side of seam

Double topstitch edge

FIGURE 5

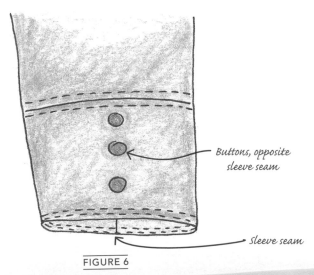

Buttons, opposite sleeve seam

Sleeve seam

FIGURE 6

make it your own!

Make this jacket your own by adding a special trim to the cuffs or detailing to the belt. Change the cuff style by using one from a different jacket variation. Make the entire jacket from a solid fabric to totally change the look.

Choose a funky home decorating fabric that's not too stiff, but also drapes well. A great stripe would also make a fun statement with this design, accented with a large fabric flower on the collar.

fabric choices

Fabrics are so fun to shop for, especially when you know something about them. Even a little knowledge can be a great help.

Most quality **cottons** are going to be found in independent fabric and quilting shops. They are almost always 44" or 45" wide. Some cotton twills (heavier weight and better suited for jackets) will be 54" wide.

Linen has a reputation for wrinkling easily, but that improves as the item is worn. Linen is wonderful to work with, so don't let a few wrinkles scare you off. These come in 54" to 60" widths, and are usually found in the dressmaking section, though sometimes you'll find them in the home decorating section.

Denims also come in 54" to 60" widths, and the content can vary. Some are 100% cotton, others will be blends of cotton and Tencel, polyester or even spandex.

Velvet and corduroy are another great fabric choice for jackets. These are usually found in 45" widths. The direction of the "nap" on these fabrics will catch the light differently, which gives the fabric a distinct directionality even though there's no print. Because of this, be careful to purchase enough fabric to cut all of the pieces in one direction.

Wools are usually 60" wide. They are best suited for jackets. Watch the labels, because most will need to be dry-cleaned.

Silk is another great fabric choice to add texture. It normally comes in widths ranging from 54"-60". Look for it in the dressmaker's or home decorating section of your favorite shop. Water can leave spots on silk, so test a small piece with the steam setting of your iron to see if you will encounter any problems. If spotting occurs, use a non-steam setting. Also remember that it is usually best to dry-clean silk. It loses sheen when washed conventionally.

Resources

Fabric

The fabrics used in this book were produced by the manufacturers listed below. Fabrics are available through these manufacturers for wholesale only, but the websites often list retailers which carry the specific lines. Because fabric lines change seasonally, you may not be able to find the exact fabric I used—but you may find something better!

Free Spirit/Westminster Fibers
3430 Toringdon Way, Suite 301
Charlotte, NC 28277
www.freespiritfabric.com
www.westminsterfabrics.com

Michael Miller Fabrics
118 West 22nd Street, 5th Floor
New York, NY 10011
www.michaelmillerfabrics.com

Moda Fabrics
13800 Hutton Drive
Dallas, TX 75234
www.unitednotions.com

Robert Kaufman Fabrics
129 West 132nd Street
Los Angeles, CA 90061
www.robertkaufman.com

Timeless Treasures Fabrics
483 Broadway
New York, NY 10013
www.ttfabrics.com

Weeks Dye Works
1510-103 Mechanical Blvd.
Garner, North Carolina 27529
www.weeksdyeworks.com

Buttons

The buttons used in the jacket section came from the manufacturers listed below.

Blumenthal Lansing
1929 Main Street
Lansing, IA 52151
www.blumenthallansing.com

JHB International
1955 South Quince Street
Denver, CO 80231
www.buttons.com

Index

What's Your Next Stitch?

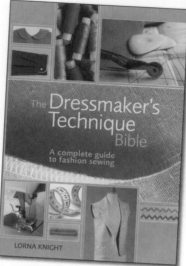

Joel Dewberry's Sewn Spaces
Fresh and Modern Fabric Projects
for Your Life and Home

Joel Dewberry

Popular fabric designer Joel
Dewberry has come up with more
than 25 projects that show you
how to use fabric to define the
spaces in your life—whether that's
where you work, play or live.

paperback, with cover envelope for tissue
pattern inserts; 9" × 9.5"; 128 pages
ISBN-10: 0-89689-924-1
ISBN-13: 978-0-89689-924-7
SRN: Z3608

The Dressmaker's Technique Bible
A Complete Guide to
Fashion Sewing

Lorna Knight

A complete resource of techniques
for designing and making clothes,
whether you're following a
pattern, adding embellishments
or designing clothes from scratch.

hardcover with concealed wire-o; 6" × 8";
256 pages
ISBN-10: 0-89689-694-3
ISBN-13: 978-0-89689-694-9
SRN: Z2316

**The Sewing Machine
Attachment Handbook**

Charlene Phillips

Rufflers, binders, hemmers—oh
my! Find out what all those
wonderful presser feet are really
for, and learn how they can produce
fabulous results in your sewing!

paperback; 8" × 10"; 144 pages
ISBN-10: 0-89689-923-3
ISBN-13: 978-0-89689-923-0
SRN: Z3607